# My First
# **Planet Earth**
# Encyclopedia

# My First
# Planet Earth
# Encyclopedia

Jen Green

# PaRragon

Bath · New York · Singapore · Hong Kong · Cologne · Delhi · Melbourne

Consultant: John Williams
This edition produced by Tall Tree Ltd, London

This edition published by Parragon in 2009
Parragon
Queen Street House
4 Queen Street
Bath BA1 1HE, UK

ISBN 978-1-4075-1268-6
Printed in China

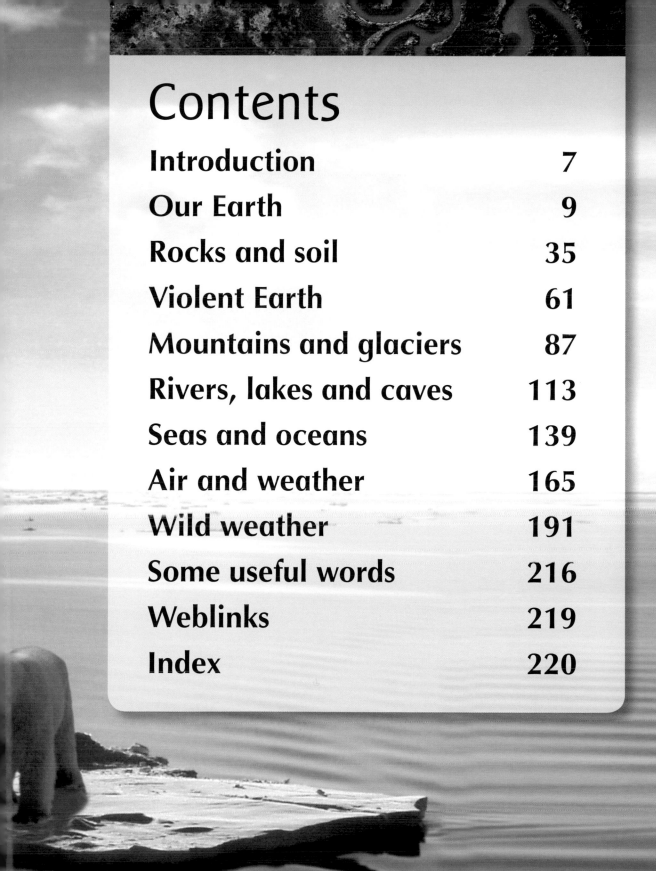

# Contents

Introduction 7

Our Earth 9

Rocks and soil 35

Violent Earth 61

Mountains and glaciers 87

Rivers, lakes and caves 113

Seas and oceans 139

Air and weather 165

Wild weather 191

Some useful words 216

Weblinks 219

Index 220

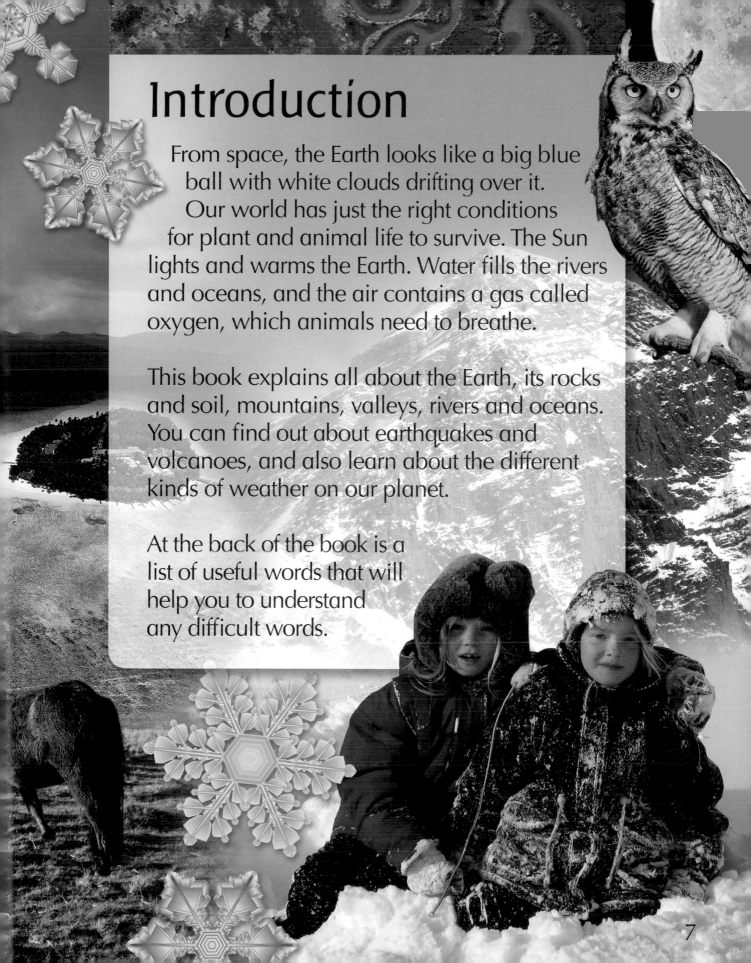

# Introduction

From space, the Earth looks like a big blue ball with white clouds drifting over it. Our world has just the right conditions for plant and animal life to survive. The Sun lights and warms the Earth. Water fills the rivers and oceans, and the air contains a gas called oxygen, which animals need to breathe.

This book explains all about the Earth, its rocks and soil, mountains, valleys, rivers and oceans. You can find out about earthquakes and volcanoes, and also learn about the different kinds of weather on our planet.

At the back of the book is a list of useful words that will help you to understand any difficult words.

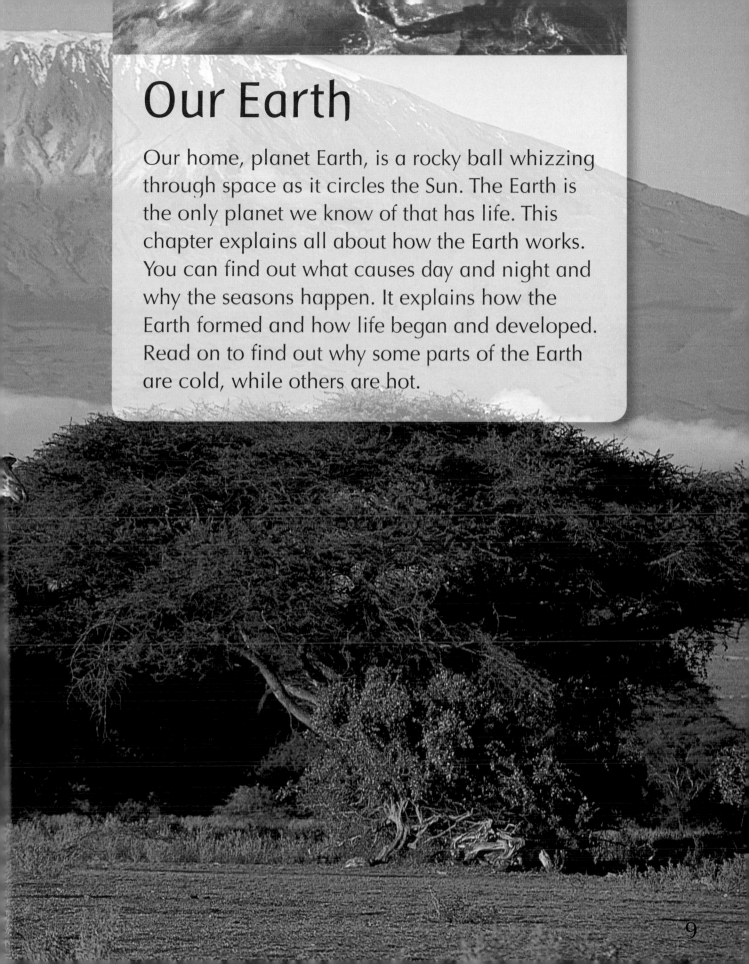

# Our Earth

Our home, planet Earth, is a rocky ball whizzing through space as it circles the Sun. The Earth is the only planet we know of that has life. This chapter explains all about how the Earth works. You can find out what causes day and night and why the seasons happen. It explains how the Earth formed and how life began and developed. Read on to find out why some parts of the Earth are cold, while others are hot.

# Our solar system

The Earth is one of eight main planets circling the Sun. The Sun, these planets and a number of dwarf planets and smaller rocks make up the solar system. The Earth and the planets follow paths called orbits as they circle the Sun.

**DID YOU KNOW?**

The Earth moves at more than 100,000 kilometres an hour as it circles the Sun. Each year, it travels nearly 940 million kilometres to complete a full circle.

## The planets

The Earth is the third planet from the Sun, after Mercury and Venus. The Earth is the fifth-biggest planet, but all the planets are tiny compared to the Sun.

Sun    Mercury    Venus    Earth    Mars    Jupiter

## The Sun

The Sun is our local star. It is an enormous fiery ball shooting light and heat in all directions. The Sun's rays light and heat the Earth. Without the Sun's warmth and energy, no living things could survive on the Earth.

## The Earth

The Earth looks blue from space because it is mainly covered by oceans. The equator is an imaginary line that divides the Earth into two halves called hemispheres. The poles are the places farthest north and south on the Earth.

North Pole

Equator

South Pole

Saturn

Uranus

Neptune

Pluto
(dwarf planet)

## Stars

All the stars in the night sky are suns, like our Sun. Believe it or not, our Sun is just one of 100 billion stars in our part of the universe. Our Sun belongs to a huge group of stars called the Milky Way.

# Spinning Earth

The Earth seems still but, in fact, our world is spinning as it circles the Sun. This spin is called rotation. It takes 24 hours to complete one full rotation, which we call a day.

## Day and night

The Earth rotates around an imaginary line called the axis, which joins the North and South poles. When the Earth turns into the sunlight, it is day where you live. When the Earth turns out of the sunlight, it is night.

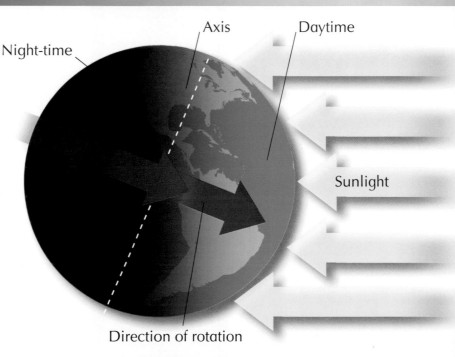

Night-time

Axis

Daytime

Sunlight

Direction of rotation

## Daytime

When the day begins, the Sun seems to rise in the east. It then moves across the sky and goes down, or sets, in the west. But the Sun isn't really moving. The Earth's rotation produces this effect.

When an object blocks the sunlight, it makes a shadow. When you wave, your shadow waves too!

## Night-time

When it is dark, your part of the Earth faces away from the Sun. The Moon and stars shine in the darkness. The Moon has no light of its own but is lit up by the Sun.

**DID YOU KNOW?** The Sun is about 150 million kilometres from the Earth. It takes just over eight minutes for sunlight to reach the Earth. Light travels at more than 300,000 kilometres per second.

## Night owls

Many people and animals are awake and busy during the day when the Sun shines and we can see clearly. Most of us sleep at night when it's dark and we can't see much, but some animals, such as owls, hunt at night.

The owl's large eyes help it to hunt in dim light at dusk or by moonlight.

# The Earth's orbit

As you sit still reading this, the Earth is racing on its journey, or orbit, around the Sun. It takes 365 days to complete one full orbit. We call this a year. The Earth tilts, and this produces the regular changes we call the seasons.

## The Earth's tilt

The Earth leans over as it rotates and orbits the Sun. This tilt carries places on the Earth nearer to or farther from the Sun at different times of year.

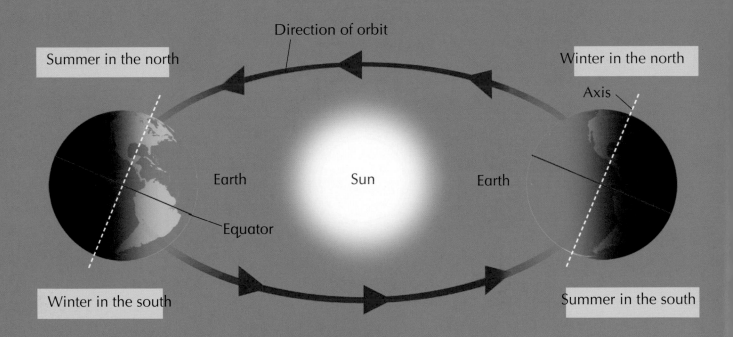

Summer in the north

Winter in the north

Direction of orbit

Axis

Earth

Sun

Earth

Equator

Winter in the south

Summer in the south

## The seasons

As the Earth orbits the Sun, the northern half of the world leans towards the Sun and has summer. The southern half leans away and has winter. Six months later, the Earth leans the opposite way, and the seasons are reversed.

**DID YOU KNOW?**

The seasons are most noticeable at the poles. This is because these parts are most affected by the Earth's tilt.

Daffodils are spring flowers.

## Spring

In spring, your part of the Earth starts to lean towards the Sun. The days get longer and the weather warms up. Flowers bloom and trees grow new leaves.

## Summer

Days are long and nights are short in summer. Your part of the Earth tilts towards the Sun. This is the hottest season.

## Autumn

In autumn, your part of the Earth begins to lean away from the Sun. Days get shorter and nights get longer. The weather grows colder.

## Winter

Winter brings long nights and short days. This is the coldest season. The part of the Earth where you live is tilted away from the Sun.

In autumn, some leaves change colour and fall off the trees.

# Forces on the Earth

The Earth's huge size and weight make it pull objects towards it. This pull, called gravity, prevents you and everything else on the Earth from flying off into space!

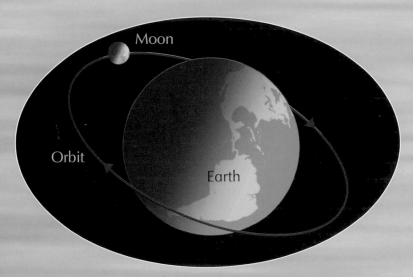

Moon

Orbit

Earth

## The Moon

The Earth's gravity keeps the Moon orbiting around it. The Moon also has gravity, which tugs at the oceans on the Earth.

## Gravity

The Earth's gravity causes anything you drop to fall to the ground. All huge, heavy objects, such as planets, have gravity. The Sun's gravity is very strong. It keeps the Earth and other planets in the solar system rotating around it.

**DID YOU KNOW?**

The area affected by a planet's magnetic pull is called its magnetic field. The Earth's magnetic field stretches 60,000 kilometres into space.

## Magnetic pull

Scientists believe that iron inside the Earth makes it magnetic – it acts like a giant bar magnet. The ends of this magnet are the North and South poles. The Earth's magnetic pull reaches far out into space.

Tiny pieces of iron called filings are pulled towards this bar magnet, showing its magnetic field.

## Which way is north?

The Earth's North and South poles have a very strong magnetic pull. A compass contains a magnetic needle that points to the north. It can be used to help people find their way if they are lost.

However high you jump on a trampoline, the pull of gravity will bring you back to the Earth!

The Sun

# How the Earth formed

The Earth is incredibly old. Scientists believe the Sun and planets began to form about five billion years ago. Our solar system developed from a cloud of gas and dust spinning in space.

## The solar system forms

Gas in the centre of the spinning cloud formed the Sun. Bits of dust stuck together to make rocks. These crashed and stuck together to make rocky planets, including the Earth. Meanwhile, the Sun's gravity kept the planets rotating around it.

Pieces of rock orbiting the Sun crashed together to form larger rocks and planets.

### Early Earth

The young planet Earth was a fiery ball of hot, liquid rock. The heat came from all the rocks that had crashed together. Heavy rocks sank to the planet's centre. Lighter rocks floated to the surface. There, they gradually cooled to make a crust.

# Rocks from space

The early Earth had no atmosphere to shield it from space. Giant rocks called meteorites crashed to the planet's surface. They made large hollows called craters.

Meteorite crater, Arizona, USA.

## The Earth facts

- The Earth's inside is still red-hot, liquid rock. The outside has cooled and hardened to make a solid crust.
- The Earth is not perfectly round. It bulges slightly in the middle and is flatter at the poles.
- The Earth is tiny compared to the Sun. You could fit more than a million Earths inside the Sun.

## Volcanoes everywhere

About four billion years ago, the Earth's surface was dotted with volcanoes (see pages 64–75) erupting red-hot melted rock, or lava. Gas and steam from the volcanoes formed the Earth's first atmosphere. The steam formed clouds, which dropped rain. The water collected in hollows, which eventually became the oceans.

19

These bacteria are shown many times larger than actual size.

# Life begins and changes

Scientists believe that life began on the Earth about 3.8 billion years ago. Over millions of years, living things very slowly changed to suit their surroundings. These changes are called evolution.

## First life

The first living things appeared in the oceans. They were tiny, simple creatures called bacteria, made of just one cell. Much later, tiny plants called algae developed in the sea.

## Plants make oxygen

The algae used the Sun's energy to grow. They gave off oxygen. Some of these tiny plants grew in mounds called stromatolites. These mounds still grow in warm seas today.

Stromatolite mounds, Australia.

## Animals appear

The first animals appeared in the oceans about 600 million years ago. They, too, were very simple creatures, with soft bodies. Gradually, animals developed more complicated bodies made up of many cells. Some, such as sea creatures called trilobites, developed hard shells.

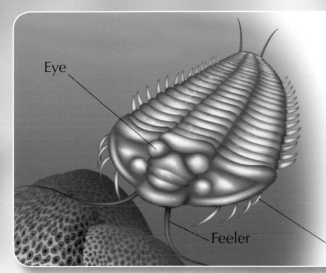

Eye

Feeler

Trilobites had many legs.

# Life moves onto land

About 400 million years ago, the first animals with backbones appeared. They were fish. Gradually, many different types of fish evolved. Some developed fleshy fins and crawled out of the water to live on land.

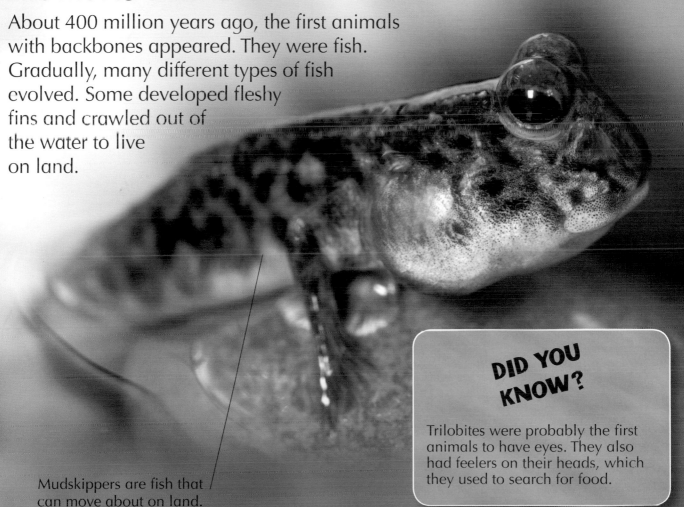

Mudskippers are fish that can move about on land.

# Fossils

Fossils are the remains of plants and animals that lived and died millions of years ago. The remains have been preserved, usually as rock. Scientists discover all about prehistoric life by studying fossils.

The hard shell of this ammonite has turned to rock.

## Ammonite

This is a fossil of an ammonite. Ammonites were creatures with shells that swam in the oceans millions of years ago. The living animal had tentacles that stuck out of its coiled shell.

## How ammonite fossils formed

When the ammonite died, it sank to the seabed. The soft parts rotted away, and the shell was buried by sand. Over millions of years, the sand slowly hardened into rock. Minerals seeped into the shell, until it too became rock.

Dead ammonite sank to the seabed.

Ammonite and sand slowly turned to rock.

## Amber

Amber is a different kind of fossil. The clear, yellow material is fossilized tree resin – a sticky sap that oozed from prehistoric trees. Insects got trapped in the sap, which then hardened to make a fossil.

You can see the insects' delicate legs and wings in this fossil.

Amber fossils may be up to 90 million years old.

## Fossil fern

The print of a fern leaf has been preserved in this rock. Ferns like warm, damp conditions. They grew well in the steamy prehistoric forests 300 million years ago.

# Prehistoric life

Since life began, many amazing animals have lived on the Earth. We call the long period from 230 million years ago to 65 million years ago the Age of Reptiles. During this time, giant reptiles ruled the land, sky and sea.

*Tyrannosaurus Rex* was a fierce meat-eating dinosaur.

## Dinosaurs

A group of reptiles called the dinosaurs were a terror on the land. There were many sorts of dinosaurs. Some were only as big as cats. Others were the size of jumbo jets. Some dinosaurs were meat-eaters, while others ate only plants.

**DID YOU KNOW?**

The largest dinosaurs measured about 22 metres long. The ground shook when they walked. The very biggest dinosaurs were plant-eaters. There are no dinosaurs living today.

Plesiosaurs swam using their feet as paddles.

## Swimming and flying reptiles

Other huge reptiles swam in the oceans. Plesiosaurs had long, snake-like necks and feet shaped like paddles. Another group of reptiles, the pterosaurs, soared through the skies on skin-covered wings.

## Dinosaur fossils

This scientist is uncovering the skeleton of a dinosaur. He is chipping away the rock to reveal the fossil. Dinosaur bones have been found all over the world. Experts also find dinosaur tracks, and even dinosaur dung.

## Dinosaurs die out

The dinosaurs and other giant reptiles died out 65 million years ago. Experts believe a giant space rock, or meteorite, smashed into the Earth, causing a huge dust cloud to block the Sun for years. As a result, many plants died and there was not enough food for the dinosaurs.

The meteorite exploded when it hit the Earth. The disaster made the Earth's climate change suddenly.

# The Earth's climate

Climate is the regular pattern of weather.
Each part of the Earth has its own climate.
The Sun has a big effect on the climate,
but so do mountains, the seas and the cities.

## Heat from the Sun

The Sun's rays are directly
overhead at the equator.
This region has a hot,
tropical climate. At the
poles, the Sun's rays
spread over a wider area,
so they have less heating
power. This means that the
poles have a cold climate.

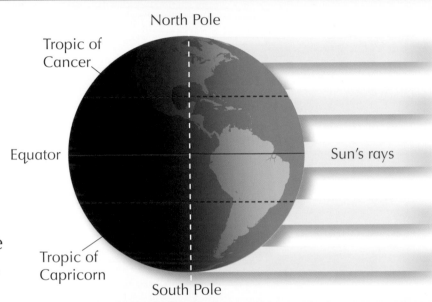

North Pole

Tropic of
Cancer

Equator

Sun's rays

Tropic of
Capricorn

South Pole

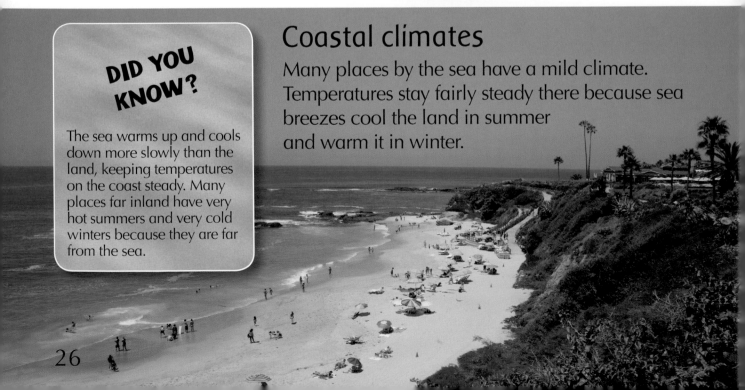

**DID YOU KNOW?**

The sea warms up and cools
down more slowly than the
land, keeping temperatures
on the coast steady. Many
places far inland have very
hot summers and very cold
winters because they are far
from the sea.

## Coastal climates

Many places by the sea have a mild climate.
Temperatures stay fairly steady there because sea
breezes cool the land in summer
and warm it in winter.

# Cool heights

Mountains usually have a cold climate. The air high on mountains cannot hold as much of the Sun's heat as the air at sea level. The tops of high mountains are covered with ice and snow all year round.

Clouds bring rain to mountains.

## City climates

Cities only cover quite a small area of the planet but have their own climate. Buildings and roads soak up the Sun's heat by day and give it out at night. This makes cities warmer than the nearby countryside.

# Climate zones

A region's climate affects the plants and animals that live there. Large areas of the Earth's surface have the same types of plants growing there. These regions are called biomes.

THE ARCTIC

NORTH AMERICA

Key to biomes

Mountains

Tropical rainforests

Temperate woodlands

Evergreen forests

Tropical grasslands

Temperate grasslands

Tundra

Deserts

Polar

SOUTH AMERICA

## The Earth's biomes

You can see the world's main biomes on this map. The types of plants that grow in each place depend on how warm it is and how much rain falls. Hot, rainy places have many types of plants. Fewer plants grow in cold or dry places.

## Deserts

Deserts are very dry places where less than 25 centimetres of rain falls each year. Some deserts get no rain at all for years. Deserts may be sandy, rocky or stony. Many are boiling hot by day and freezing cold at night.

EUROPE

ASIA

Tropic of
Cancer

AFRICA

Equator

Tropic of
Capricorn

AUSTRALASIA

ANTARCTICA

Temperate
woodland in autumn.

## Temperate zones

Temperate regions lie
between the poles and
the tropics and have
a mild, rainy climate.
In temperate woodlands,
most trees lose their
leaves in autumn.

## Cold forests
## and tundra

In the cold northern forests,
trees stay green all year. Little
grows in the icy tundra except
during the short summer.
The ground beneath the
surface stays frozen all year.

Plants bloom during
the short tundra summer.

29

# Hot climates

Places on the equator and in the tropics have hot climates. It is warm there all year round, and nights are never frosty. Snow only falls on the tops of the very highest mountains.

Death Valley is a desert in western USA.

## Hottest places

Dallol in East Africa has the hottest average temperature on the planet – it stays at about 34 degrees Celsius. Death Valley, USA, has some of the highest temperatures ever recorded – up to 56 degrees Celsius – but it does not stay that hot all year round.

## Two seasons

The climate in the tropics is not affected by the Earth's tilt, so there is no spring, summer, autumn or winter. But some tropical places have two seasons – a dry and a rainy season.

India has its wet season from April to September every year.

## Lush rainforests

Rain falls almost every day on most places at the equator. Rainforest trees love the hot, damp conditions. More types of plants and animals live in tropical rainforests than in any other biome.

## Hot grasslands

Tropical grasslands grow in places that get less rain than rainforests but more rain than deserts. These areas are home to many grass-eating animals, such as zebras and antelopes, and the animals that feed on them, such as lions.

**DID YOU KNOW?**

In 1922, the city of Al Aziziyah in North Africa had the highest temperature ever recorded on the Earth. It was an incredible 57.7 degrees Celsius.

Lions live on the tropical grasslands in Africa.

31

The Sun shines all night in summer at the poles.

# Cold climates

The regions surrounding the north and south poles are the coldest places on the Earth. The Sun's rays have little warmth there. Most land in the polar regions is covered by a thick layer of ice and snow.

## Shimmering lights

Swirling curtains of light sometimes shimmer in the night sky at the poles. These beautiful lights are called auroras. The lights may be red, green or purple. This amazing display is caused by particles from the Sun hitting gases high in the air.

## Midnight sun

In summer, each pole tilts towards the Sun. At night, the Sun dips low in the sky, but never sets. So it stays light, even at midnight. In winter, the pole leans away from the Sun. The Sun never fully rises, so it is dark all the time.

## The Arctic

The area around the North Pole is called the Arctic. This region is mainly an ice-covered ocean. Polar bears and seals live in the sea and on the ice.

This polar bear is hunting seals on the ice.

Penguins have thick feathers and a warm, fatty layer under their skin.

## Antarctica

The area around the South Pole is called the Antarctic. The vast icy land of Antarctica lies in this area. Antarctica is covered with a thick cap of ice up to three kilometres deep. No animals live inland, but penguins and seals live on the coast.

# Rocks and soil

This chapter explains how rocks form and how the rocks at the surface are broken down by rain, wind, frost and sunlight. Underground, there are many riches, such as gold, silver and diamonds. Valuable fossil fuels – coal, oil and gas – come from beneath the ground too. But soil, which lies on top of the Earth's rocky surface, may be the greatest treasure of all. Read on to find out why.

# Rocky planet

We live on the Earth's hard, rocky surface called the crust. Deep below the crust, the rocks are hot – so hot they are melted and flow like sticky treacle.

## Inside the Earth

Scientists believe the Earth is made of several layers. The surface crust is thin. Below the crust is a thick layer called the mantle, with red-hot rocks. In the core at the centre, the rocks are hotter still.

Inner core

Outer core

Crust

Mantle

Cross-section through the Earth

The Earth's rocky crust at the Grand Canyon, USA.

# Heat from below

Deep mines are hot because of the hot rocks below. But even the very deepest mines are just like a pinprick in the giant rocky ball that is the Earth.

This man is working in a hot, deep mine.

Thin crust

Ocean

Land

Thick crust

# Rocky crust

Cliffs and mountains are formed from the Earth's crust. If you stripped away the grass, soil or concrete at any place on the Earth, you'd hit rock. These cliffs were made by a river cutting through the rock.

# Ocean crust

The Earth's crust is thicker beneath the land than beneath the oceans. The crust beneath the land is 20 to 90 kilometres thick. Beneath the oceans, it is only about seven kilometres thick.

## DID YOU KNOW?

Scientists believe the temperature at the centre of the Earth is more than 5000 degrees Celsius. The outer core is made of partly liquid rock. The inner core is a solid ball of metal.

# Fiery rocks

Rocks form in different ways. Fiery rocks come from deep underground. Red-hot, liquid rock bubbles up to near the surface, then cools to form solid rock.

## Glowing lava

Red-hot, liquid rock deep underground is called magma. When it spills on to the surface at a volcano (see pages 64–75), it is called lava. Lava cools and hardens quickly at the surface.

### Frothy pumice

A type of rock called pumice was once frothy lava. Like froth on a fizzy drink, it contains air bubbles. The bubbles were trapped when the lava cooled. Bubbles make this rock so light it floats on water.

People use pumice to rub away hard skin while bathing.

## Giant's Causeway

Basalt is a hard fiery rock. Volcanoes on the seabed erupt melted basalt. The red-hot lava cools quickly when it hits the water. The Giant's Causeway in Northern Ireland is made of basalt pillars. These formed when the lava cooled quickly, shrank and cracked.

Six-sided basalt pillars

**DID YOU KNOW?**

The rocky pillars at the Giant's Causeway mainly have six sides. Legend says a giant laid the rocks as stepping stones.

A granite building in Scotland.

## Granite

Granite is another hard fiery rock. It forms where magma rises but cools before it reaches the surface. This hard stone is used for making buildings and roads.

# Wearing away

The rocks at the surface are battered by rain, wind, frost and sunshine. Bits of rock flake off and are carried away by wind and water. This process is called erosion.

This flat slab of limestone is criss-crossed with deep grooves.

## Eating into rock

Rainwater contains a weak acid that eats into soft rocks such as limestone. This is similar to when an aspirin dissolves in water. The rainwater slowly wears deep grooves in the rock.

## Shattered by ice

In cold places, such as on mountainsides, water seeps into cracks in the rock and freezes at night. Ice takes up more space than water, so the ice widens the cracks. Eventually, the rock flakes away.

Ice has made this rock crack.

# Worn by wind

In dry, windy places, sand and grit are carried on the wind. When the wind blasts against rock, the sand and grit act like sandpaper. This can carve smooth curves into the rock.

This rock in Western Australia is called Wave Rock.

## Carried away

When it rains, trickling water carries away small pieces of loose rock. The water drains into streams and rivers, which carry the rocky pieces downhill. They end up in seas or lakes.

# Settled-down rocks

Fiery rocks are not the only type of rock. Another type forms from rocky pieces that are carried out to sea by rivers. The pieces get squashed together by more rocky fragments and eventually turn into solid rock.

## Rock layers

When the rocky pieces are carried out to sea, they settle in layers on the seabed. Later, the rock layers may be pushed upwards when mountains form (see pages 90–91) and become part of the land.

You can see the rock layers in this sandstone cliff in New Zealand.

## Clay pots

Clay is a rock that is soft when wet. Potters shape clay to make pots. The pots are baked in an oven to make them hard.

These children are helping to make a clay pot.

## Puddingstone

A rock called conglomerate contains round pebbles that settled on the seabed. When the layer was squashed, the pebbles stuck together. The rock is also sometimes called puddingstone because it looks like pudding mixture.

These cliffs are made of chalk.

## Chalk

Chalk is a soft, white rock made of the tiny shells of millions of sea creatures. The shells built up on the seabed and were later buried. The shelly layer very slowly turned to chalk. This rock can be used to draw on blackboards and pavements.

45

# Changed rock

Changed rocks are another type of rock. They form when rocks are heated or squeezed below ground. The rocks may be squeezed by other rocks on top of them, or they may be squeezed by magma rising upwards, which can also heat the rock.

## Heated rock

This is a changed rock called gneiss. The wavy lines show where the rock layers have been melted and squeezed. Sometimes squeezing happens when rocks shift underground during earthquakes (see pages 76–85).

## Slate

Slate forms when a rock called shale is squashed deep below ground. Slate naturally splits into thin sheets that make great roof tiles.

44

## Marble

Marble forms when limestone rock is heated underground. Heating and squeezing make the rock change colour and texture. Marble can be carved easily and its surface polished until it shines.

## The Taj Mahal

The Taj Mahal is a beautiful palace in northern India. It is made of white marble and decorated with coloured marble. Marble comes in several colours – black, pink, green and white. Some marble has swirling patterns.

The dome is made of marble blocks of different colours.

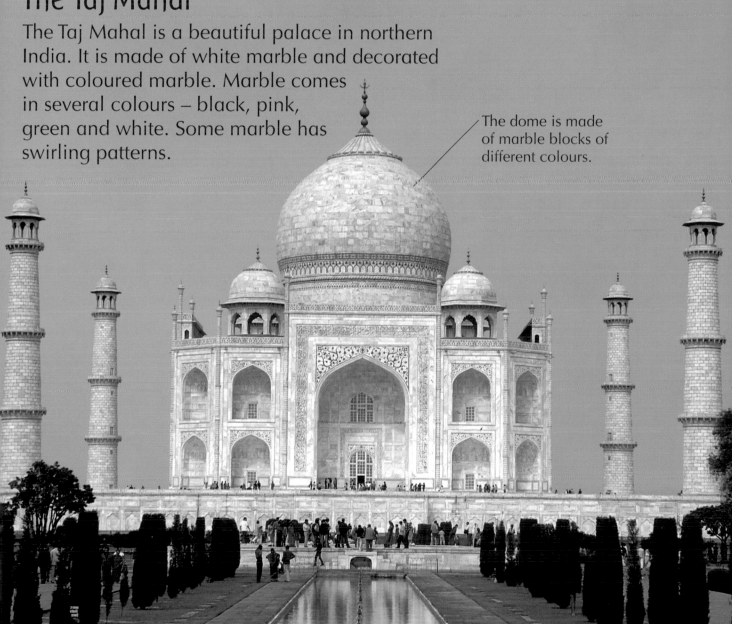

# Bryce Canyon

Bryce Canyon is a national park in western USA. It is formed of layered rocks called sandstone, limestone and mudstone. Over time, water, ice and wind have carved fantastic shapes into the rocks.

## Wildlife park

Animals such as deer and foxes live in Bryce Canyon. Some use the rocks for shelter. There are also birds, such as swallows, ravens and eagles.

## Hoodoos

The tall rock spires of Bryce Canyon are called hoodoos. These rocky pillars are made of soft mudstone topped with harder limestone. Ice and water wear the soft mudstone away more quickly than the harder cap of rock.

Water, ice and wind wear grooves in the rock.

## Bryce Canyon facts

- The rocks of Bryce Canyon formed on the beds of lakes and rivers. Over millions of years, the forces that build mountains lifted these rocks 2500 metres above sea level.

- Bryce Canyon has more hoodoos than almost any place on the Earth.

A bald eagle's wings can measure 2.5 metres across.

## Colourful rocks

The rocks of Bryce Canyon are pink and orange. The minerals iron and manganese give the rocks their colour. At sunrise and sunset, the rocks glow bright red.

## Rock arch

Thunderstorms and hailstorms can strike Bryce Canyon in summer. Snow and ice cover the ground in winter. Rain, hail, snow and ice wear away the rocks to make amazing features like this arch below.

### DID YOU KNOW?

Bryce Canyon became a national park in 1928. The park covers 145 square kilometres. The hoodoos of Bryce Canyon are up to 60 metres tall.

49

# Minerals

Rocks are made of natural materials called minerals. There are thousands of different minerals but only about a hundred are common.

Feldspar

Mica

Quartz

## Granite

Granite is made up of three different minerals – quartz, mica and feldspar. They can be seen in this close-up photograph. Granite is used as building stone.

## Plaster from gypsum

If you break an arm or a leg, the doctor will put a plaster cast on it while it heals. Plaster is made of a soft mineral called gypsum. The wet plaster sets to make a hard cast.

Wet plaster is moulded around the leg.

**DID YOU KNOW?**

A soft mineral called graphite is used to make the lead in pencils. Crayons and paints can be made using another soft mineral called talc.

## Copper mines

Valuable minerals, such as copper, are dug from mines. Many mines run deep below ground, but copper is often found near the surface. Copper is used to make water pipes and electrical wire.

## Fireworks

Fireworks, such as sparklers, are made from a yellow mineral called sulphur. Sulphur is also used to make matches and explosives. Next time you see a firework display, remember sulphur!

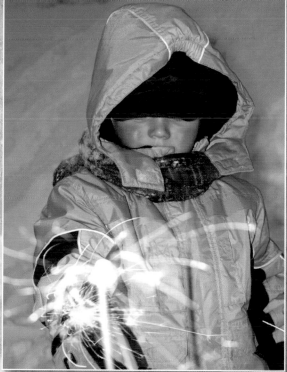

49

# Metals

Strong, shiny metals can be worked into different shapes. Metals are found in rocks called ores, often mixed with other minerals. Rare metals, such as gold, are expensive.

Lump of gold ore

Gold wedding ring

## DID YOU KNOW?

The largest gold nugget ever found weighed 70 kilograms. It was found in Victoria, Australia, in 1869. The lump was nicknamed the Welcome Stranger!

## Gold

Gold is usually found in rocks deep below ground. But a few lucky people have found whole lumps, called nuggets, at the surface! Specks of gold are sometimes washed out of rocks by water, and are found on river beds.

## Silver

Silver is another rare metal found in an ore. Ores are usually crushed and heated to get the metal out. In the past, silver was sometimes used to make coins.

These silver coins come from Ancient Greece.

## Gold rush

When someone discovers gold, thousands of people rush to the same area, hoping to get rich. This is called a gold rush. Gold in river gravel is collected by swirling the gravel around in a pan. The gold sinks to the bottom. This is called panning.

A miner panning for gold in California, USA, in 1890.

## Making iron

Iron is made by heating iron ore in a hot furnace, or oven. Limestone and coke (a type of coal) are also added. Hot, liquid iron runs out at the bottom of the furnace. Iron is used to make an even stronger metal called steel.

Red-hot, runny iron flows from the furnace into a container.

# Gems and jewels

Minerals called gemstones can be made into jewels. Experts cut and polish the gems until they sparkle. There are more than 50 different sorts of gemstones. They are all rare, but some are very rare.

## Rough diamond

A diamond forms when a material called carbon is heated and squeezed very hard underground. Diamonds do not have much sparkle when they come out of the ground. Many sides are cut into the gem to make it sparkle.

Uncut diamond

**DID YOU KNOW?**
Diamonds are the hardest mineral found on the Earth. They are used to make cutting tools as well as jewels.

This diamond has been cut and polished so it sparkles.

52

## Crystals

Most gemstones form as even-sided crystals. Each type of crystal has a regular shape with a certain number of sides. You can see the large, purple crystals in this chunk of amethyst.

## Many colours

Gemstones come in many beautiful colours. Sapphires are blue, emeralds are bright green and rubies and garnets are dark red. Opals have many colours. They are not cut with many sides but are smoothed and rounded.

Most large opals come from Australia.

## Crown jewels

The crown of the British king or queen has more than 3000 jewels! One of the largest stones is a famous diamond called the Cullinan II Diamond. The largest red stone is called the Black Prince's Ruby.

# Fossil fuels

Most of the energy we use at home comes from coal, oil and gas. They are formed from fossils – the remains of prehistoric plants and animals. That's why we call them fossil fuels.

## Coal mining

Coal is usually found deep below ground in layers called seams. A deep hole called a shaft is dug to reach the coal. Coal is burned in power stations to produce electricity for homes and factories.

A lump of coal

Ferns and trees grew in prehistoric forests.

Dead plants were squashed to make peat.

Peat slowly turned to coal.

## How coal was made

Coal formed when prehistoric plants from swampy forests died and sank into the swamp. They were squashed as soil and rock built up on top and slowly hardened into peat, a type of soil. The peat then slowly hardened into coal.

## Oil and gas

Oil and gas are the remains of tiny sea creatures that were buried and squashed on the seabed. They slowly turned to oil and gas. These fuels are mined from the seabed by drilling deep holes. Oil is made into petrol for cars. Gas is used for cooking and heating.

Cars burn fuel to power their engines.

**DID YOU KNOW?**

When cars, factories and power stations burn fossil fuels, they give off waste gases that cause pollution. The pollution is making the world's climate warmer. Find out more about this on pages 212–213.

## Made from oil

Oil has many uses. Plastic and nylon are made from the leftovers when oil is purified. Paint, lipstick and candles are also made from oil.

All these plastic objects are made from oil.

# Soil story

You may not think of soil as valuable. But in a way, soil is even more precious than gold, oil or diamonds. Plants need soil to grow, and animals need plants for food. So most living things depend on soil.

Humus

Topsoil

Subsoil

Bedrock

## Soil layers

Soil contains several layers. At the very top is a thin layer of rotting plants called humus. The rich topsoil contains plant and animal remains. The subsoil below contains broken rocks. At the bottom is solid bedrock.

## How soil is made

Soil is made from tiny bits of rock mixed with plant and animal remains. Soil begins to form when ice, water and wind break rocks into pieces. Plants take root in the rocky pieces. Rotting plants and animal remains make the soil richer.

## Tree roots

Trees spread their roots through the soil. The roots draw water and nourishing minerals from the soil. They also anchor the tree in windy weather. Roots break up rocks to form more soil.

## Different soils

There are many types of soil. Sandy and chalky soils are dry and powdery. Clay soil is sticky. Different plants like different types of soil. Gardeners need to choose the right plants for the soil in their garden.

### DID YOU KNOW?

It takes hundreds of years to form even a thin layer of soil. Soil is much deeper in some places than others – it may be anything from a few centimetres to several metres deep.

# Life in soil

Soil contains thousands of different living things, from tiny insects and spiders to earthworms and larger animals, such as moles and rabbits. The crops that provide our food grow in soil.

## Animal burrows

Earthworms and moles burrow in the soil. Their tunnels let air and water in. This helps to make the soil more fertile. Worms and moles spend their lives under the ground.

## Eat and be eaten

Living things in the soil depend on one another for food. Earthworms feed on rotting leaves. Moles feed on earthworms. When animals die, their remains nourish the soil, which helps more plants to grow.

Moles shovel away the soil using their powerful front claws.

These oxen are pulling a plough in India.

## Ploughing the soil

Farmers prepare the soil for growing crops by ploughing. This turns the soil over and helps air and water reach the lower layers. The plough can be pulled by a tractor or by animals, such as oxen or horses.

This combine harvester is pouring ripe grain into a truck.

## Harvest time

Farmers harvest crops when they have grown and ripened. Some farmers cut the crop by hand. Others use a machine called a combine harvester to cut and gather the crop.

# Violent Earth

Volcanoes and earthquakes are two of nature's scariest wonders. Rivers of hot, melted rock gush from an erupting volcano. Ash, rocks and gas blast high in the air. During an earthquake, the ground heaves and houses, trees and bridges collapse. Earthquakes and volcanoes happen because of powerful forces underground. Read on to find out when, where and why earthquakes strike and volcanoes erupt.

# The Earth's crust

The Earth's hard outer crust sits on top of red-hot, squishy rock. The crust is not one solid layer but is made of giant slabs of rock. The huge slabs are called plates.

These yellow lines show the edges of the Earth's plates.

## Moving plates

The Earth's plates fit together like pieces in an enormous jigsaw puzzle. Currents in the melted rock below cause the plates to drift very slowly. These movements produce earthquakes and volcanoes on the Earth's surface.

## Faults

As the Earth's plates move very slowly across the surface, they bump and scrape one another. Where two plates scrape together, a long crack called a fault sometimes appears.

A fault at the point where two plates meet in Iceland.

## Volcanoes

The Earth's crust is thin and weak where the plates meet. Red-hot, melted rock wells up from below, breaks through and spills out onto the surface. We call these places volcanoes (see pages 64–75).

## Earthquakes

Plates moving past each other sometimes jolt violently. The jolt, which makes the ground shake, is called an earthquake (see pages 76–85). Earthquakes can do great damage.

An earthquake has made this building in Japan collapse.

**DID YOU KNOW?**

The Earth's plates move very, very slowly. They shift about 2.5 centimetres each year. People's fingernails grow at about the same rate.

# Volcanic eruptions

When melted rock, called lava, spills out of a volcano, it is called an eruption. Lava rushes out in fiery rivers, then cools to form solid rock. It slowly builds up in layers to form a mountain.

## Inside a volcano

Red-hot rock inside the Earth is called magma. Magma builds up below the volcano in a magma chamber. As more magma rises, the pressure builds up. Red-hot lava, ash, gas and steam burst out through the top of the volcano.

Ash

Crater

Magma

Magma chamber

## Flying rocks

Some volcanoes shoot chunks of red-hot rocks high in the air. The hot rocks fly through the air and then splatter on the ground. These deadly rocks are called lava bombs.

Lava shoots out of the crater of a volcano in Hawaii.

## Hollow crater

The opening in the top of the volcano is called the crater. As the eruption dies down, the large hole gets blocked by ash and solid lava. These shoot out with great force the next time the volcano erupts.

— Lava

## Glowing clouds

During some eruptions, clouds of burning ash pour out of the volcano. These heavy clouds spill down the mountain, moving much faster than lava. They burn anything in their path.

A huge cloud of ash erupts from Mount Mayon, a volcano in the Philippines.

# Types of volcano

The shape of a volcano depends on the type of lava that spills out of it. The two main types of volcanoes are tall, cone-shaped volcanoes and flatter shield volcanoes.

## Underwater volcanoes

Some volcanoes erupt under the sea. The hot lava cools as soon as it hits the water. This forms rounded lumps of rock called pillow lava.

## Cone-shaped volcanoes

Some volcanoes explode violently, throwing out thick, sticky lava. This type of lava flows only a short way before cooling and turning solid. Layers of lava and ash build up to form a cone-shaped mountain.

A cone-shaped volcano in the Philippines.

A shield volcano on the islands of Hawaii.

## Shield volcanoes

Some volcanoes erupt runny lava. This lava flows a long way before cooling and turning solid. A low, rounded hill called a shield volcano eventually forms.

Snow covers the top of a dormant volcano in Africa.

## Sleeping volcano

Not all volcanoes erupt all the time. A volcano that has not erupted for a long time but may erupt again is called a dormant volcano. 'Dormant' means 'sleeping'. A volcano that has stopped erupting is called an extinct volcano.

67

# Mount St Helens

In May 1980, a volcano called Mount St Helens in western USA suddenly erupted. The whole top of the mountain blew off in a violent explosion.

## Before the eruption

Mount St Helens had not erupted for 123 years before the 1980 eruption. The mountain looked peaceful, but inside the pressure was slowly building.

## Whoosh!

When Mount St Helens erupted, ash, gas and steam escaped with an enormous 'whoosh'. People living hundreds of kilometres away heard the explosion. A thick layer of ash rained down on the countryside.

## Wrecked forests

Forests of tall trees covered the lower slopes of Mount St Helens before the eruption. The blast snapped the trees like matchsticks.

### Eruption facts

- The cloud of ash from Mount St Helens rose 20 kilometres in the sky. The ash made the sky dark and drifted on the wind to settle over a wide area. Towns up to 300 kilometres away were covered in ash.
- Mount St Helens erupted violently for four days. Smaller eruptions continued for several months afterwards.

## New life

After the eruption, Mount St Helens looked lifeless. Ash lay thick on the ground and choked lakes and rivers. After just a few months, plants began to sprout and animals returned to Mount St Helens.

# Famous eruptions

The most powerful eruptions do a lot of damage. When water or snow mixes with volcanic ash, it produces a tide of mud, which can destroy towns and villages.

A model of a dog made by pouring plaster into a hollow in the ash.

## Mount Vesuvius

About 2000 years ago, a volcano called Vesuvius erupted in southern Italy. The Roman town of Pompeii was buried under a thick layer of ash and was not discovered again for hundreds of years.

## Buried by ash

When hot ash rained down on Pompeii, many people died. The bodies of some people and animals left behind hollow spaces in the hard ash.

# Deadly ash

In 1991, Mount Pinatubo on the Philippines erupted, and ash covered the landscape. Heavy rain turned the ash to mud, which swept across the island. Several villages were buried by the mud.

STA BARBARA ELEMENTARY SCHOOL

## Tide of mud

In 1985, the Nevado del Ruiz volcano high in the Andes Mountains in South America erupted. Red-hot lava and ash melted snow on the mountain. A tide of mud roared downhill and buried the town of Armero in the valley below.

# Volcanic wonders

The heat from volcanoes creates amazing volcanic landscapes, which include hot springs and mud pools. The soil around volcanoes also makes good land for growing crops.

## Hot springs

In hot springs, the water is heated by hot rocks underground. People like to bathe in the warm water. Some monkeys in Japan bathe in hot volcanic springs to keep warm during the icy winter.

Monkeys at the hot springs in Nagano, Japan.

## Useful volcanoes

Volcanic rock and ash break down to make rich soil for farming. This farmland is on the slopes of a volcano in the Philippines. Coconut trees and rice grow well in the fertile volcanic soil.

In Yellowstone National Park, USA, a geyser shoots a jet of water every 72 minutes. The geyser is called Old Faithful. The hot fountain can shoot up to 40 metres high.

Steam from this geyser erupts high into the air.

## Bubbling mud

In some volcanic areas, water mixes with hot ash to make pools of bubbling mud. The mud is rich in minerals. Some people put volcanic mud on their faces and bodies because they believe it is good for their skin.

## Hot fountain

Water trickling underground may be heated by hot rocks. When the water reaches boiling point, it shoots upwards, like steam shooting from a kettle. The fountain of hot water is called a geyser.

Fireproof suit
and mask protect
the scientist.

## Volcano experts

Scientists who
study volcanoes are
called volcanologists.
A volcanologist is taking
a sample of lava from
an eruption on Hawaii
to learn more about
the volcano.

# Studying volcanoes

Nothing can stop a volcano from
erupting. But experts can often tell when
a volcano is about to erupt. They warn
people to leave if they are in danger.

## Gas samples

These scientists are taking gas
samples from a volcano. If there is
more gas than usual, it may mean
that the volcano is about to erupt.
One volcanic gas, sulphur
dioxide, smells like rotten eggs.

74

## Time to go

When people have to leave because a volcano is about to erupt, it is called an evacuation. These people are evacuating the island of Montserrat in the Caribbean because of danger from a nearby volcano.

## Keeping watch

If an eruption is coming, gas and steam may start to leak from a volcano. The mountain may bulge as melted rock builds up inside. The scientist, below, is checking the shape of Mount St Helens in 2004 to make sure it is still safe.

**DID YOU KNOW?**

Some volcanoes still fool the experts by erupting without warning. In 1973, a volcano in Iceland suddenly started to spout red-hot lava. Everyone had thought the volcano was extinct!

This huge crater was made by the 1980 eruption.

# Earthquakes

The plates that form the Earth's crust are always moving slowly. This puts the rocks below ground under great strain. An earthquake happens when the rocks suddenly jolt into a new position.

Epicentre is the point on the surface directly above the focus.

## Shock waves

Earthquakes usually start deep underground. The point where rocks grind and shatter is called the focus. Shock waves spread out in all directions. The damage is worst on the surface directly above.

Shock waves

Focus

A building torn apart by the force of an earthquake.

## Wrecked buildings

Powerful earthquakes make the ground shake. Buildings can be torn from their foundations. Glass shatters and steel beams bend like rubber. Houses sway and crash to the ground.

**DID YOU KNOW?**

Thousands of earthquakes strike each year, but most are tiny. Small quakes make lightbulbs swing and ornaments rattle. The most powerful earthquakes wreck whole towns.

# Cracked ground

When an earthquake strikes, the violent shaking can make the ground split open. Huge cracks can appear in roads and pavements. Some cracks are big enough to swallow cars!

# Broken bridge

Strong earthquakes can damage roads and bridges. In 1995, an earthquake in Japan destroyed this motorway. Wrecked roads and railways can make it difficult for outside help to reach a region hit by an earthquake.

This crack appeared in a road after an earthquake in California in 1989.

# Effects of earthquakes

An earthquake lasts only a few seconds, but the shaking can do terrible damage. Earthquakes also start fires, cause landslides and turn solid ground to mud.

## Fire!

Fires start when gas pipes and electricity lines are damaged by earthquakes. In 1989, fire swept through San Francisco, USA, after an earthquake. Water pipes were damaged by the earthquake, making it difficult for firefighters to put out the flames.

## Dam burst

Powerful earthquakes can destroy dams built on rivers. A wall of water then bursts through the dam and rushes downriver. Towns and villages lower down get swept away. This dam in Taiwan was wrecked by an earthquake in 1989.

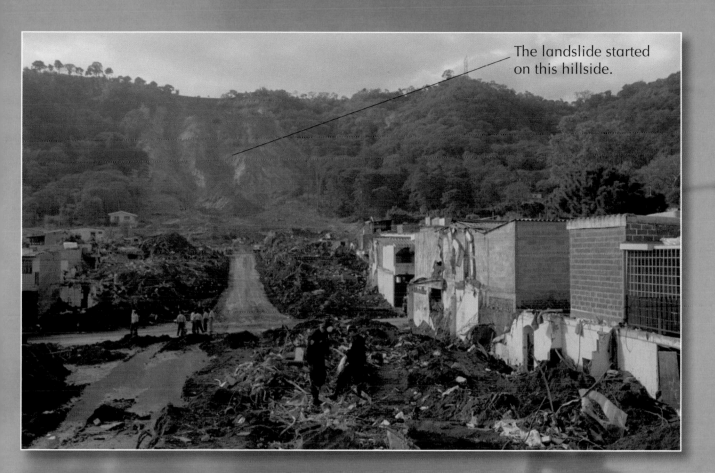

The landslide started on this hillside.

## Landslide

When the ground shakes, loose soil and rock can slip away in a landslide. This landslide happened after a quake in Central America in 2001.

## Sinking ground

Violent shaking can turn clay or sandy soil to mud. Buildings sink into the mud or topple over. These blocks of flats collapsed after an earthquake hit Niigata in Japan in 1964.

79

# Tsunamis

Earthquakes can strike under the sea as well as on land. When an earthquake shakes the seabed, it can cause enormous waves called tsunamis. These waves race across the ocean and wreck towns when they reach the coast.

## 2004 tsunami

In December 2004, a strong earthquake rocked the seabed off Indonesia in Southeast Asia. Giant waves spread out like ripples. The waves travelled nearly 5000 kilometres to wreck towns on the shores of India and even Africa.

India

Thailand

Africa

Maldives

Sri Lanka

Malaysia

Indonesia

Indian
Ocean

Key to map

━━ Areas hit by the tsunami    ● Epicentre    ◎ Waves spreading outwards

All the buildings in this town in Indonesia were destroyed by the 2004 tsunami.

## Krakatoa

Volcanic eruptions can also cause tsunamis. In 1883, a volcano on an island called Krakatoa, near Indonesia, exploded. The explosion set off tsunamis that spread far and wide. The waves swamped coastal towns, and 36,000 people died.

### DID YOU KNOW?

When Krakatoa exploded, the bang was heard 5000 kilometres away. The explosion destroyed most of the island, but fresh flows of lava formed a new island. The new island was named *Anak Krakatoa*, which means Child of Krakatoa.

## Towering waves

Out to sea, tsunamis form low waves that aren't very noticeable. They build up to become much taller when they reach shallow water. The huge waves are a terrifying sight when they smash onto the shore.

## Wrecked coast

Damage from the 2004 tsunami was worst on the coast of Indonesia. Whole towns were completely flattened by the waves. Boats were swept onto the shore and carried far inland.

# Deadly earthquakes

Earthquakes can be incredibly destructive. The damage is often worst in cities, where many people are killed by falling buildings. Earthquakes have brought disaster to many parts of the world.

**DID YOU KNOW?**

San Francisco lies on a fault where two plates scrape past each other. This fault runs for 1200 kilometres along the coast of western USA. Earthquakes have struck San Francisco quite often – in 1906, 1989 and again in 1994.

## Lisbon, 1755

In 1755, an earthquake struck out to sea near the city of Lisbon in Portugal. Huge waves wrecked Lisbon's harbour. Candles burning in churches and houses were knocked over and fires started all over the city.

## San Francisco, 1906

In 1906, a powerful earthquake wrecked the city of San Francisco in the USA. Fires broke out and raged for days because firefighters ran out of water.

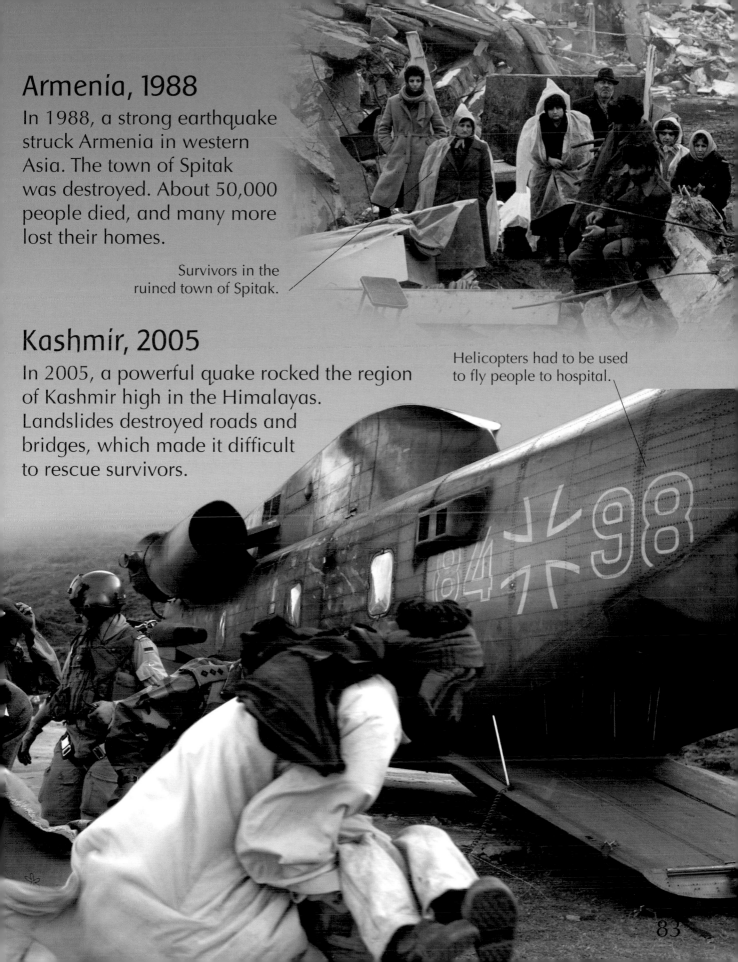

# Armenia, 1988

In 1988, a strong earthquake struck Armenia in western Asia. The town of Spitak was destroyed. About 50,000 people died, and many more lost their homes.

Survivors in the ruined town of Spitak.

# Kashmir, 2005

In 2005, a powerful quake rocked the region of Kashmir high in the Himalayas. Landslides destroyed roads and bridges, which made it difficult to rescue survivors.

Helicopters had to be used to fly people to hospital.

# Watching earthquakes

Scientists use machines to measure the strength of earthquakes. If experts believe an earthquake is due, they warn everyone. But it is very hard to say exactly when and where an earthquake will strike.

Bigger zigzags show bigger quakes.

**DID YOU KNOW?**

In 1975, scientists in the Chinese city of Haicheng noticed animals acting strangely. They gave the order for everyone to leave the city. A few hours later an earthquake struck.

## Measuring quakes

A seismograph measures the shaking caused by earthquakes. Pens fixed to weights hang above a roll of paper. When an earthquake strikes, the paper shakes, and the pens draw zigzags on the paper.

## Animal warnings

Animals often act strangely just before an earthquake. Rats run away, while cats miaow and dogs bark. Some experts believe that animals can hear the very high, faint noises made by rocks that are stretched to breaking point before the quake.

The pyramid shape of this building helps it stay upright in an earthquake.

## Safety practice

If an earthquake strikes, people should stay indoors and hide under a strong desk or table. This Japanese child is practising what to do in an earthquake. She is wearing a padded hood to protect her head.

## Safer buildings

In areas where earthquakes are likely, people design buildings that will cope with the shaking. This tall building in San Francisco has strong steel beams to support it.

# Mountains and glaciers

Mountains are the highest places on the Earth. This chapter explains how these rocky peaks form and describes some of the plants and animals that live there. Read on to find out about mountain dangers and about living in, and visiting, these high places. This chapter also explains what glaciers are and how they form.

Snow-covered K2 is
8611 metres tall.

# Towering mountains

Mountains are high, rocky areas
that rise above their surroundings.
Many mountains have steep,
sloping sides, and the tops of
very high mountains are cold
and covered with snow.

## Mountain chains

Some mountains stand alone, but many
form long lines called chains or are found in
groups called ranges. The Andes in South
America is the longest mountain chain on
land, stretching for 7200 kilometres.

South
America

Andes

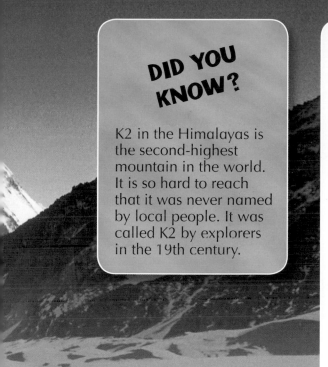

## DID YOU KNOW?

K2 in the Himalayas is the second-highest mountain in the world. It is so hard to reach that it was never named by local people. It was called K2 by explorers in the 19th century.

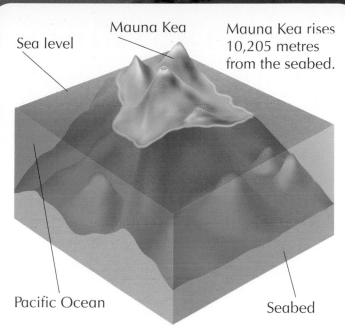

Sea level

Mauna Kea

Mauna Kea rises 10,205 metres from the seabed.

Pacific Ocean

Seabed

## Rising from the ocean

Mountains are usually measured from sea level. Mauna Kea, a mountain in Hawaii, rises 4205 metres above the surface of the sea, but the rest of the peak lies underwater. Mauna Kea is taller than Mount Everest when measured from the seabed.

## The Himalayas

The Himalayas in southern Asia are the world's highest mountains. This mighty range includes Mount Everest, which at 8863 metres is the Earth's highest mountain on land.

## Africa's highest peak

Mount Kilimanjaro is the tallest peak in Africa. This mountain rises to 5895 metres. The top is covered with snow even though Kilimanjaro is near the equator, where the climate is hot.

89

# Fold mountains

Many of the world's highest mountains are found in places where two plates of the Earth's crust push against each other. Rocks are pushed upwards, forming fold mountains.

Fold mountains in the Pyrenees in Spain.

## How fold mountains form

Fold mountain ranges form where two of the Earth's plates crash together. The land in between the plates is pushed up and the rocks fold, forming mountain peaks. The Himalayas in Asia and the Pyrenees and the Alps in Europe are fold mountain ranges.

**1.** The Earth's plates push together.

**2.** Rocks are pushed up.

**3.** Range of fold mountains forms.

# Zigzag rocks

As the layers of this rock in the UK were squashed, they folded to form these amazing zigzag patterns.

## DID YOU KNOW?

The Alps and Himalayas are still rising as rocks are pushed upwards. In about 1000 years, these mountains will be about a metre taller than they are today.

# Volcanic mountains

Volcanoes are another type of mountain. These form when hot, melted rock erupts on to the Earth's surface. Layers of erupted rock build up to make tall, cone-shaped mountains.

Cotopaxi is a volcanic mountain in Ecuador, South America.

# Blocks and domes

Two other types of mountains are steep-sided block mountains and rounded dome mountains. All mountains take millions of years to form, but some are much older than others. Young mountains are usually much higher than old mountains.

The Tetons in North America are block mountains.

## Block mountains

The movement of the Earth's plates sometimes causes long cracks called faults to appear (see page 62). If a huge slab of rock is pushed upwards between two faults, it makes a steep-sided peak called a block mountain.

## How block mountains form

This diagram shows how blocks of rock are pushed upwards between faults to form mountains. If a block of land slips down between faults, it forms a deep, flattish valley. This is called a rift valley.

Rift valley

Block mountain

Faults

92

## How dome mountains form

Dome mountains form where hot, melted rock pushes up but cools before it reaches the surface. The layered rocks on top are pushed up into a dome shape. Later the rocks on top wear away to reveal the dome of volcanic rock.

Layers of rock

Dome of volcanic rock

## Worn smooth

Mountains are slowly worn away by the weather. Over millions of years, high, jagged mountains become lower and smoother. Ben Nevis (left) in Scotland is a very old dome mountain with a rounded top.

# Mount Everest

At 8863 metres tall, Mount Everest is the world's highest mountain. This famous peak lies in the Himalayas, on the border between Nepal and Tibet in China. The mountain's local name, Chomolungma, means 'mother goddess of the world'.

Snow covers the bare, rocky slopes of Mount Everest.

**DID YOU KNOW?**

Lhotse, the world's fourth-highest mountain, lies very close to Everest. The two mountains are linked by a snowy ridge.

## Climbing Everest

The first climbers to reach the top of Everest were Edmund Hillary from New Zealand and Tenzing Norgay from Nepal in 1953. Since then many others have climbed the mountain even though it is difficult and dangerous.

94

## Mount Everest facts

- The height of Everest was first measured by surveyors in the 1800s. They named it after Sir George Everest, a famous British surveyor.
- Italian Reinhold Messner was the first person to climb Everest alone and without using bottled oxygen to help him breathe.
- More than 2000 people have reached the top of Everest.

## Sherpas

Sherpas are mountain people that live in the Everest region in Nepal. These people are used to the cold and are very fit. Some work as mountain guides and others carry loads up the steep slopes.

Sherpas balance heavy loads on their backs.

## Sherpa town

Namche Bazaar is the biggest village near Everest. Sherpas live there. Not long ago the village was tiny, but now climbers and walkers stay there on their way to Everest. Namche Bazaar has become a busy town.

# Cliffs and crags

Rain, wind and ice can carve mountains into amazing shapes, including steep cliffs, uneven craggy rocks and tall, rocky pillars.

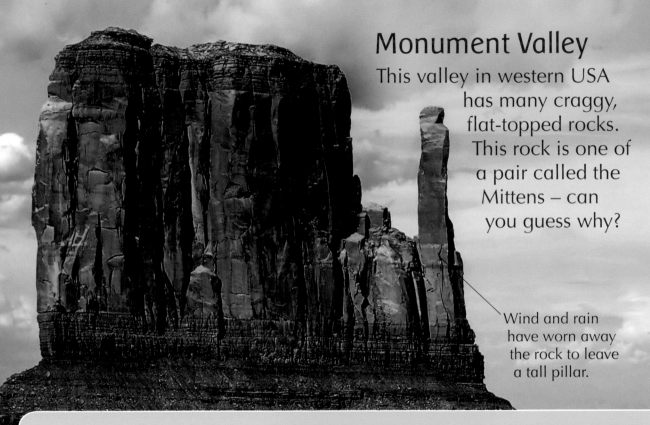

## Monument Valley

This valley in western USA has many craggy, flat-topped rocks. This rock is one of a pair called the Mittens – can you guess why?

Wind and rain have worn away the rock to leave a tall pillar.

## Devil's marbles

These amazing rocks are found in the Tanami Desert in Australia. It is very hot there in the day and freezing at night. The heat and the cold make the rocks flake. This has formed rounded shapes that look like giant marbles.

# Uluru

This mass of sandstone rock in central Australia is called Uluru. The 348-metre-tall rock is all that is left of a mountain range that once covered the area.

# Dartmoor tors

Rocky hills called tors are made of a hard fiery rock called granite. Frost and rain crack the rocks and help form the craggy shapes. Many tors are found on Dartmoor in southern England.

# Mountain habitats

Mountains have extreme weather conditions with long, icy winters. The weather is often windy, rainy or snowy. Mountain plants and animals have to be tough to cope.

## Brrrrr!

Mountain air is thinner (contains less gas) than air in the lowlands. Thin air can hold less of the Sun's heat, so the higher up you climb the colder it gets.

People who live on or visit the mountains have to wear warm clothes to keep out the cold.

Snowy peak

Grassy meadows

Treeline

Forest

## Mountain plants

Different plants grow at different heights on mountains. Trees only grow on lower slopes. At the top, no plants can grow, and snow covers the bare rock. On the middle slopes, there are grassy meadows filled with flowers.

Trees do not grow on mountains above a point called the treeline.

## Mountain animals

Animals that live high on mountains have thick hair to keep them warm. Birds have extra-warm feathers. This llama lives in the Andes. Llamas have large lungs that help them breathe the thin mountain air.

### DID YOU KNOW?

Animals called marmots live on high mountains in many parts of the world. They stay there all year, spending the winter sleeping in their burrows. This is called hibernation.

## Moving up and down

These goat-like animals, called chamois, live in the Alps. They move up the mountain to eat grass in summer. In autumn, they move down to the valley to shelter there throughout the cold winter.

Rubbery hooves grip the slippery rocks.

# Mountain dangers

Living in or visiting mountain regions can be dangerous. Sometimes, extreme weather may cause rocks or snow to break loose and roar down the mountain.

## Landslides

In 2005, houses on this hillside in California, USA, were swept away by a landslide. Heavy rain caused chunks of rock on the hillside to become loose and fall downhill.

**DID YOU KNOW?**

People who are not used to being high up on a mountain can get mountain sickness. They may get a headache and feel sick and dizzy. The cure is to go lower down the mountain.

## Avalanche!

An avalanche is when a mass of snow slips down a mountain. Loud noises or even people skiing can set off an avalanche. The snow gathers speed and roars downhill at up to 300 kilometres an hour.

## Preventing avalanches

These fences have been built to protect a village in the Alps from avalanches. The fences keep the snow in place. The danger is greatest when deep snow starts to melt in spring.

## Mountain rescue

If someone is buried by an avalanche, rescuers have to work very quickly. Dogs can be used to sniff out the person. Then rescuers use spades to remove the snow.

Rescue dogs use their good sense of smell to find people buried in avalanches.

# Using mountains

People use mountains in many different ways. Farmers grow crops or rear animals on steep hillsides. Miners dig valuable minerals from the rocks. But most mountain regions have few towns because of the harsh conditions.

## Farming

Farmers grow crops such as potatoes and rice, which can cope with the tough conditions. Low walls are built on steep slopes to make flat fields called terraces.

Rice is being grown in terraces on this steep hillside.

## Animals

Farmers rear animals such as sheep, yaks, goats and llamas for their meat, milk and wool. These animals will graze on slopes that are too steep and stony for farming.

Yaks are used to carry heavy loads in the Himalayas.

102

# Mountain village

Most mountain villages are built in sheltered valleys, not on windy mountaintops. But extreme conditions can still make life difficult for mountain people. This village is in the Himalayas region of Nepal.

## Mining in mountains

Gold, silver and copper are found in some mountains. Miners dig deep tunnels, like this one in a silver mine, to find the rocks that contain the precious metal.

**DID YOU KNOW?**

El Alto in Bolivia is one of the world's highest towns. It stands 4100 metres up in the Andes Mountains in South America. La Paz, the capital of Bolivia, is the world's highest capital at 3600 metres.

# Visiting the mountains

Some people visit mountains to enjoy the beautiful scenery and amazing wildlife. Others like to climb the steep mountainsides or ski down snow-covered slopes.

## Winter sports

Skiing and snowboarding are popular sports in winter. People visit ski resorts, which have safe, snowy slopes and lifts to carry them up the mountain. It takes a lot of practice to become a good skier!

## Hiking

Hiking is a great way to see fantastic mountain scenery. Some hikers carry a tent and all their food in a backpack. Others stay in mountain huts. These backpackers are climbing in the Pirin Mountains in Bulgaria.

## Transport

Steep slopes make travel difficult in the mountains. Roads run along the valleys or zigzag up to high passes. Cable cars carry people up very steep slopes or from peak to peak.

A cable car to Sugar Loaf Mountain, Brazil.

## Spotting wildlife

Some people visit mountains to see wildlife, such as birds or butterflies, or flowers in springtime. Parks have been set up in many mountains to protect rare plants and animals, such as the mountain gorillas in Africa.

**DID YOU KNOW?**

Tunnels have been blasted right through some mountains to build roads and railways. A tunnel under Mont Blanc, Europe's highest peak, runs for 11.5 kilometres.

Tourists watch a mountain gorilla in Congo, Africa.

# Icy glaciers

Glaciers are found in high mountains. They are rivers of ice that move very slowly downhill, scraping off pieces of rock as they flow.

## How do glaciers form?

On high mountains, snow does not melt but builds up into a thick layer. The snow underneath gets squashed down and turns to ice. The ice gets so heavy and slippery that it starts to slide downhill.

## At the end

At the lowest end of the glacier, the ice begins to melt because the air there is a bit warmer. Any pieces of rock carried along in the ice are dumped at the end of the glacier.

Deep cracks form where the ice splits.

## Oetzi, the ice man

In 1991, two climbers found the remains of a prehistoric man in a glacier in the Alps. The man had died while on a mountain journey 5000 years ago. His body had been preserved by the ice. He was named Oetzi after the valley where he was found.

This is what Oetzi may have looked like.

## Joining together

Pieces of rock are carried along the sides of glaciers, forming dark stripes called moraines. When smaller glaciers join together, the stripes meet in the middle – as can be seen in this Swiss glacier (right).

The Aletsch glacier in Switzerland is the longest in Europe.

# Worn by glaciers

Glaciers used to cover much more of the Earth than today (see pages 110–111). When these glaciers melted, they left scenery shaped by ice, including U-shaped valleys and steep-sided fjords.

**DID YOU KNOW?**

Most glaciers flow very slowly, moving 1–2 metres a day. The Quarayaq Glacier in Greenland flows much faster – more than 20 metres a day.

## Sheer sides

This tall, pointed peak was carved by glaciers flowing down all sides of the mountain. It is called the Matterhorn and is found in the Alps in Switzerland.

## U-shaped valleys

As a glacier flows downhill, it acts like a giant bulldozer. The ice gouges out a deep valley with a flat bottom. Rocks and boulders carried along beneath the glacier scrape away more soil and rock.

A glacier carved this deep, U-shaped valley in Wales.

# Mountain tarns

Small, round lakes called tarns were carved by glaciers. The ice gouged out bowl-shaped hollows high up on mountains. When the ice melted, the hollows filled with water.

A cruise ship visits a steep-sided fjord in Norway.

# Fjords

Fjords are steep-sided valleys at the coast. They were carved by glaciers thousands of years ago. Later the ice melted, and the sea rose to flood the valleys, creating fjords.

# Ice caps

In very cold places, the snow never melts. Packed-down snow builds up to form a thick layer of ice called an ice cap. In the past, ice covered much more of the Earth's surface than it does today.

North America

Arctic ice cap today

Asia

Europe

Australia

Antarctic ice cap today

South America

Africa

## Polar ice

Thick ice covers the land at the Arctic and Antarctic (see page 33). In winter, the icy area gets bigger as the sea freezes over. In summer, the sea ice melts, and the icy area shrinks again.

Ice samples, or cores, contain ice from lower layers.

## Old ice

The Antarctic ice cap is up to four kilometres deep. The ice at the bottom is made of snow that fell hundreds of years ago. Scientists study the old ice to find out what conditions were like all those years ago.

## Ice Ages

During long, cold periods called Ice Ages, ice covered much of Europe and North America. This map shows the area covered by ice in the last Ice Age, which ended about 10,000 years ago.

Arctic ice cap 18,000 years ago

Compare this with the map opposite, showing the Arctic ice cap today.

## Woolly mammoth

Huge, hairy elephants called mammoths lived in Asia, Europe and North America during the last Ice Age. Bodies of mammoths have been found in the ice in northern Russia. When the Ice Age ended, mammoths died out.

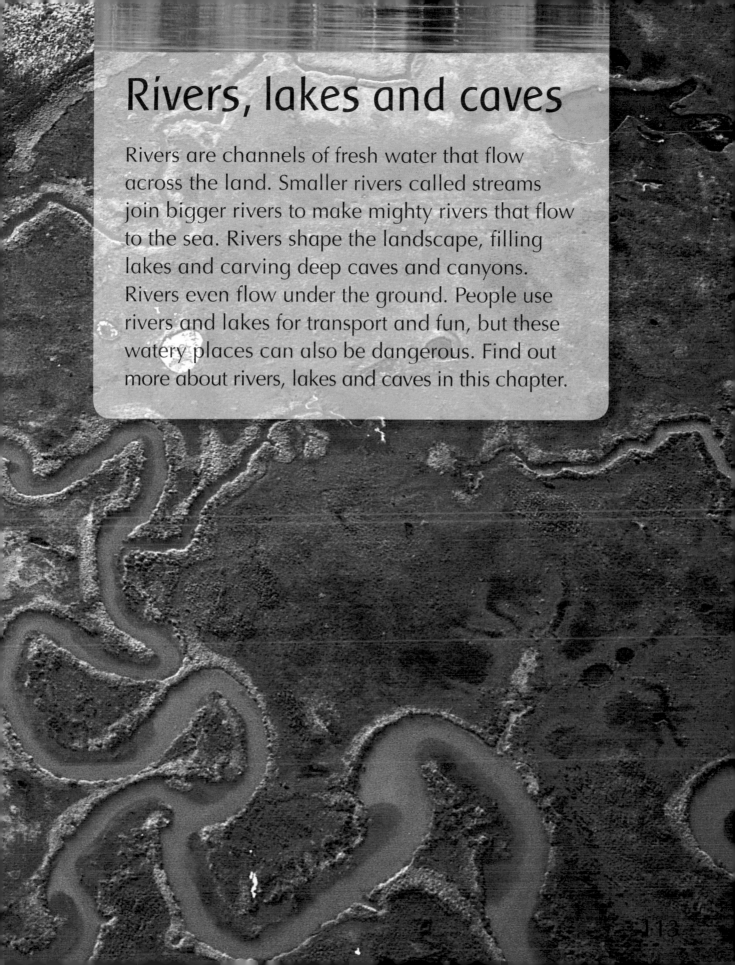

# Rivers, lakes and caves

Rivers are channels of fresh water that flow across the land. Smaller rivers called streams join bigger rivers to make mighty rivers that flow to the sea. Rivers shape the landscape, filling lakes and carving deep caves and canyons. Rivers even flow under the ground. People use rivers and lakes for transport and fun, but these watery places can also be dangerous. Find out more about rivers, lakes and caves in this chapter.

# A river's journey

A river's course is the long journey that it takes from where it begins, high in hills or mountains, to where it ends – in the sea or a lake.

## The source

The place where a river starts is called the source. The water comes from rain or melted snow. It may bubble up out of the ground at a spring or trickle out of a lake or glacier.

A stream trickles down a mountain.

## Course of a river

In its upper course, a river rushes down from a hill or mountain, carving deep gorges and valleys. In its middle and lower courses, a river makes wider valleys and creates flat areas called floodplains.

Lake

Spring

Tributary

Upper course

Middle course

Lower course

Floodplain

## Wearing and shaping

As rivers flow downhill, they carry loose stones and rocks along with them. The stones bounce along the bottom of the river and scrape more soil and rocks away.

A bear walks across the rocks and stones left by a mountain river.

## Joining the river

Trickles of water join to make streams. Streams join to make rivers. Lower down, small rivers called tributaries join the main river. The water gets wider and deeper.

# Young rivers

At its upper course, a river is known as a young river as it flows downhill. The rushing water loosens rocks and soil, carving deep canyons and gorges.

## The Grand Canyon

Canyons form where water cuts through hard rock. The Grand Canyon is a famous canyon in the USA. The Colorado River has worn a very deep valley as it has cut down through the rock.

## Deepest gorge

A gorge is a steep-sided canyon. The Kali Gandaki Gorge in the Himalayas is 5.5 kilometres deep – the deepest gorge in the world. The river has cut a deep valley between two mountains.

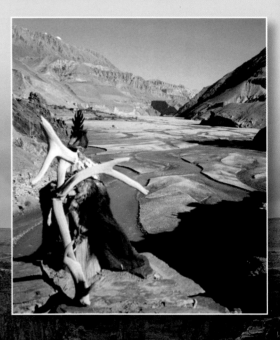

The deep valley of the Grand Canyon.

# Leaping salmon

Salmon swim up young mountain rivers to lay their eggs. They have to swim very hard against the flow of water. When they reach fast-moving water, they leap out of the water to move upstream.

These salmon are leaping up a waterfall.

**DID YOU KNOW?**

The Grand Canyon is up to 1.6 kilometres deep and 30 kilometres wide in places.

## Foaming rapids

Rapids form where young rivers plunge over stones and boulders. The white, foaming water rushes along very quickly. It is fun to ride the rapids in a rubber boat.

# Waterfalls

Where a river plunges over a steep cliff, it forms a waterfall. Beautiful falls with white, foaming water can be seen on rivers in many parts of the world.

This boat takes tourists to see the waterfall up close.

## Niagara Falls

Niagara Falls is a famous waterfall in North America. It lies on the border between the United States and Canada. The falls curve around like a giant horseshoe and are 55 metres high.

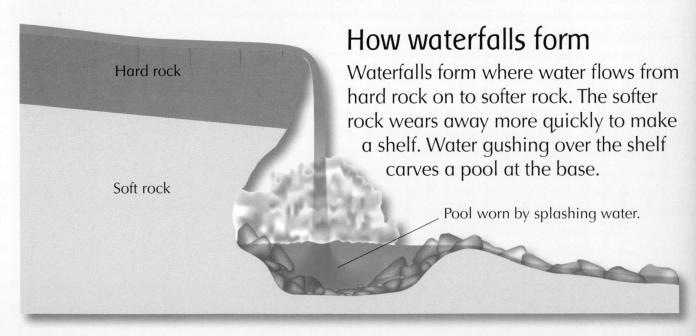

Hard rock

Soft rock

Pool worn by splashing water.

## How waterfalls form

Waterfalls form where water flows from hard rock on to softer rock. The softer rock wears away more quickly to make a shelf. Water gushing over the shelf carves a pool at the base.

# Angel Falls

Angel Falls in Venezuela, South America, is the world's highest waterfall. It is 970 metres tall and is located were the River Churún plunges over a steep cliff.

## DID YOU KNOW?

Angel Falls is named after American pilot Jimmy Angel, who spotted the waterfall from his plane in 1933.

## Iguacú swifts

Iguacú Falls is a very beautiful waterfall in South America. It is four kilometres wide and drops nearly 100 metres. Small birds called swifts nest on the rockface behind the falls. The birds fly through the water to get to their nests.

# In the valley

In the middle and lower parts of its journey, the river leaves the hills behind and flows through a wide, flattish valley.

## Fertile soil

A river carries mud and gravel. After heavy rain, the river may flood and spill muddy water on to the surrounding land – the floodplain. Crops grow well in the fertile soil of the floodplain.

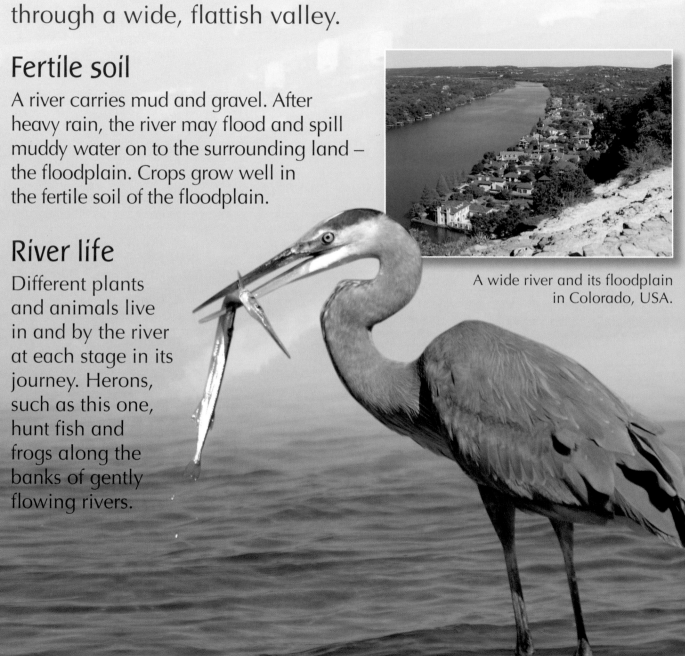

A wide river and its floodplain in Colorado, USA.

## River life

Different plants and animals live in and by the river at each stage in its journey. Herons, such as this one, hunt fish and frogs along the banks of gently flowing rivers.

River loops are called meanders.

## Twisting and turning

Rivers twist and turn as they flow through wide valleys. Water flows fastest on the outside of bends, cutting the bank away. Mud is dropped on the inside, where the flow is weaker. In time, gentle curves become deep loops.

Fastest river flow

1.

Loop

River cuts into the outside of bends.

River cuts through the loop.

2.

Oxbow lake forms.

## Oxbow lakes

Over many years, the loops get bigger and bigger. In the end, the river cuts right through the loop. The cut-off part becomes a small lake called an oxbow lake.

RUSSIA

KAZAKHSTAN

Caspian Sea

AZERBAIJAN

TURKMENISTAN

IRAN

# Lakes

Lakes are hollows in the ground filled with water from rivers or melted ice. Some hollows were carved by glaciers. Others formed because of movements in the Earth's crust.

## Largest lake

The Caspian Sea, left, is the world's largest lake. It covers 371,000 square kilometres in western Asia. Because the lake contains salty water, it is really an inland sea.

## Deepest lake

Lake Baikal in Russia is the world's deepest lake. It is more than 1700 metres deep in places. This lake is home to the only type of seal that lives in fresh water – the Baikal seal.

# Highest lake

Lake Titicaca in Peru is the highest lake in the world that boats sail on. It lies 3100 metres up in the Andes Mountains. Local people travel in boats such as this, made of bundles of reeds.

## Crater lakes

Some lakes form when water fills the crater of a volcano. Crater Lake (below) in Oregon is 592 metres deep. It is the deepest lake in the United States.

Pink flamingoes feeding in an estuary.

# Reaching the sea

The place where a river meets the sea is called its mouth. The river's flow slows as it reaches the sea, and it drops its load of sand or mud to form flat areas called estuaries or deltas.

## River estuary

The estuary is the lower part of a river, where fresh water mixes with salty seawater. Worms and snails burrow in the muddy banks, providing plenty of food for birds.

## Deltas

A delta forms when mud or sand builds up at a river's mouth. The delta may be triangular or shaped like a bird's foot. The river divides into many smaller channels as it flows through the delta.

The delta of the Mississippi River, USA, is shaped like a bird's foot.

124

## Nile Delta

The River Nile has a huge, fan-shaped delta. Mud dumped by the river has made a triangle of fertile land. Green fields are surrounded by desert, which looks brown.

**DID YOU KNOW?**

The world's largest delta is the Ganges Delta in Asia. It covers 75,000 square kilometres and has 400 kilometres of coastline.

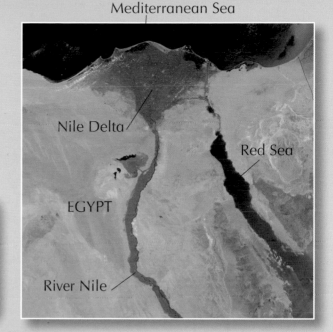

Mediterranean Sea

Nile Delta

Red Sea

EGYPT

River Nile

## Nile crocodile

In the past, the Nile Delta was home to the Nile crocodile. Now farms cover the delta, and these fierce beasts are rarely seen there. They are still found in rivers, estuaries and deltas in other parts of Africa.

# The mighty Amazon

The River Amazon in South America is not as long as the Nile, but it contains far more water. The river begins high in the Andes Mountains and flows through the Amazon rainforest on its way to the sea.

## Amazon facts

🌐 The Amazon flows for 6450 kilometres. The river and its tributaries cover more than seven million square kilometres – more than a third of South America.

🌐 The Amazon empties 150,000 cubic metres of water into the ocean every second. That's enough to fill 75 Olympic-sized swimming pools.

## River basin

Water from an area ten times the size of France flows into the Amazon. The total area through which a river and its tributaries flow is called the river's basin.

## Amazon Delta

The Amazon measures about 300 kilometres across as it reaches the ocean. The river is so wide that it looks like the sea. This picture shows water weaving between islands in the Amazon Delta.

## Flooded forest

During the rainy season, the Amazon bursts its banks and floods the surrounding forest. This canoe is skimming over what was once the river bank. The floods last up to six months of the year.

## Amazon wildlife

Piranhas are small fish that live in the river. They have razor-sharp teeth and prey on wounded fish and animals that fall into the water.

If a piranha loses a tooth, a whole new set grows.

# Underground rivers

Water flows under the ground as well as over it. Water running under the ground can wear away some types of rock to make deep, dark caves.

Gaping Gill, a sinkhole in England, is 111 metres deep.

## Disappearing water

Water eats into a type of soft rock called limestone. Over time, it makes deep holes called sinkholes and runs under the ground. The water wears away the rock beneath the surface, forming hollow caves.

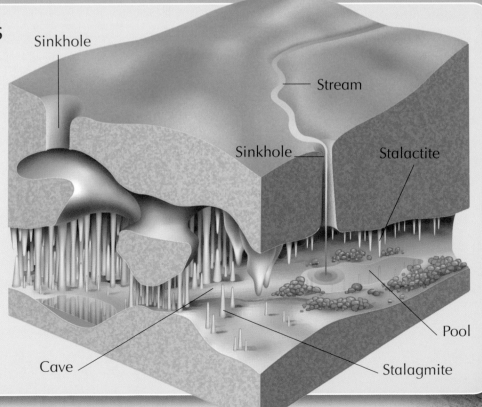

### Limestone caves

Water can form huge caves in limestone rock, linked by underground tunnels. Water falling through sinkholes can carve out deep pools. Rock formations called stalactites and stalagmites (see page 130) are often seen in caves.

Sinkhole

Stream

Sinkhole

Stalactite

Pool

Cave

Stalagmite

# Wells

If you dig down deep enough anywhere on the the Earth, you will reach water. People dig holes called wells and drop buckets down them to bring water to the surface.

# Desert oasis

Water cannot soak through all types of rock. When it reaches a layer of rock it cannot pass through, water runs sideways. Sometimes the water reaches the surface again and bubbles out in a spring. In a desert, such a place is called an oasis.

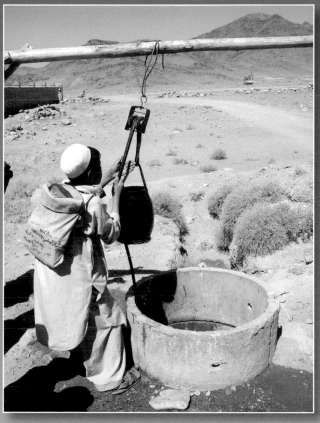

A boy draws water from a well in Afghanistan, Asia.

An oasis in Libya, Africa.

129

# Amazing caves

In some places on the Earth, a secret world lies underground, where caves and tunnels run for kilometres. Exploring this hidden world is called potholing.

Stalactites hang down from the ceiling.

## Stalagmites and stalactites

Stalagmites and stalactites are stony pillars found in caves. They are made by dripping water. The water contains a mineral called calcite, which builds up to make the pillars.

Stalagmites rise from the floor.

## Potholers

Potholers wear waterproof clothes and a helmet with a light on when they explore these dark, wet places. This potholer is looking at a stalactite.

## Bat caves

Many bats like dark places. They sleep in caves by day and hunt for food at night. Bats hang upside down from cave walls using their sharp claws.

## Cave paintings

In prehistoric times, some people lived in caves. They painted pictures of the animals they hunted on cave walls. This painting in a French cave is more than 15,000 years old.

### DID YOU KNOW?

The largest group of linked caves and tunnels is the Mammoth Cave System in Kentucky, USA. The caves run for 560 kilometres.

# Using rivers

Rivers provide water for drinking, washing and cleaning. People also use rivers to water crops, run factories and make electricity. No wonder people live beside rivers all over the world.

## Water for farming

River water is vital for farming. These green fields beside the River Nile are watered by the river. Without the Nile, this place would be a desert.

## Cities on rivers

Most of the world's oldest towns and villages were built beside rivers. Some of these are now capital cities, such as London and Paris. The Houses of Parliament (below) in London are next to the River Thames.

# Water for energy

Hydroelectric stations use energy from fast-flowing water to make electricity. A dam is often built to control the flow of water. This is Glen Canyon Dam in Arizona, USA.

# Factories by rivers

Factories of all kinds use river water to power machinery, and also for cleaning. Paper mills, like this one, use huge amounts of water every day.

**DID YOU KNOW?**

Glen Canyon Dam is 216 metres high. A huge lake called Lake Powell has built up behind the dam. The lake supplies water to nearby cities.

# Travel and fun

Rivers have been used by people to travel or move goods ever since boats were invented. Rivers and lakes are also great places to have fun.

## River transport

Paddleboats like this one have sailed the Mississippi River, USA, since the early 1800s. They carry passengers and cargo. This boat is taking tourists on a sight-seeing trip.

## Canals

Canals are human-made waterways. People dig canals to link rivers, lakes or seas. In Central America, the Panama Canal cuts across a narrow strip of land to link the Pacific and Atlantic oceans.

Huge cargo ships on the Panama Canal.

## Crossing rivers

In some places, bridges have to be built to carry road and railway traffic over rivers. This bridge in Bristol, western England, crosses the River Avon. Vehicles have to pay a fee to use the bridge.

## Water sports

Rivers and lakes are used for many sports, such as canoeing, sailing, fishing and even windsurfing. This boy is paddling a type of canoe called a kayak.

**DID YOU KNOW?**

The world's longest bridge is the Akashi Kaiko Bridge in Japan. It links two islands and is nearly four kilometres long.

# River safety

Rivers can be dangerous places.
Floods can strike after heavy rain,
damaging roads and houses. Dirty river
water can also harm people and animals.

These people are
stacking sandbags
to try to keep
the Mississippi
floodwater away
from their homes.

## Mississippi floods

In 1993, the Mississippi River in the USA
burst its banks. Floodwater covered more than
44,000 square kilometres. About 70,000
people had to leave their homes.

## Floods in China

When the Yangtze River
in China flooded in 1998,
this family escaped by
boat. Sadly, more than
3000 people died and
about 14 million were
made homeless.

In China, the Yellow River is called 'China's sorrow' because it has caused such bad flooding. In 1938, 90,000 people died when the river burst its banks.

## Water pollution

River water can be polluted (made dirty) by sewage or waste from farms and factories. This can harm people. Many countries now have strict rules to stop river pollution.

This pipe is emptying dirty water into a river.

## Preventing floods

During very high tides (see pages 142–143), seawater could flood London. The Thames Barrier was built to protect the city. It has huge gates that can be shut to prevent seawater flowing into the river.

# Seas and oceans

The oceans are a vast world that we are still exploring and finding out about. This chapter will explain how waves, tides and currents affect the ocean and shape the land. It will tell you how coasts, islands and coral reefs form. You can also find out about the creatures that live at different depths in the oceans, including the deep sea – a mysterious world that we know very little about.

# Watery world

Only a third of the Earth's surface is land. Salty water covers the rest. This huge expanse of water is divided into areas called oceans and seas.

## Salty oceans

Ocean water is salty because it contains minerals carried out to sea by rivers. The main minerals are sodium and chloride. These two minerals make salt.

**DID YOU KNOW?** The Pacific Ocean is the world's biggest ocean. It covers 166 million square kilometres and holds over half of all the water in the oceans.

Warm current  Cold current
Arctic Ocean
NORTH AMERICA
EUROPE  ASIA
Atlantic Ocean
AFRICA
Pacific Ocean
SOUTH AMERICA
Indian Ocean
AUSTRALASIA
Southern Ocean
ANTARCTICA

## Oceans and seas

The five oceans are called the Atlantic, Pacific, Indian, Arctic and Southern oceans. They are linked by smaller areas of water called seas. Warm and cold currents flow like mighty rivers through the oceans.

### Super-salty water

The Dead Sea in Asia is seven times saltier than other seas and oceans. The salt makes the water thicker, so it is easier to float. But all that salt means that nothing lives in the Dead Sea – that's how it got its name.

## Warm waters

A warm current called the Gulf Stream warms the coasts of Britain and Ireland. The current starts near Mexico and flows across the Atlantic Ocean.

Palm trees grow in the mild climate on western Irish coasts.

# Waves and tides

The water in seas and oceans is always on the move. Waves sweep across the ocean surface. The sea rises and falls on coasts as tides come and go.

## How do waves form?

Winds blowing across the ocean make ripples on the surface. The ripples grow into waves. Far from land, low waves roll across the ocean. Waves get taller as they reach the coast.

## Circling water

The water in a wave moves in a circle. Far out to sea, the water circles freely. Close to shore, the seabed stops water flowing in circles. This makes the waves rise up into crests.

Crest

Beach

Wave breaking on shore

Circling water

142

# Changing tides

Tides mainly happen because the Moon's gravity (see pages 16–17) pulls on the oceans. As the Moon circles the Earth, it pulls the sea towards it. A mound of water forms below the Moon – this mound is high tide.

A surfer rides a huge wave.

## High and low tides

These pictures show the same harbour in Cornwall, England, at high and low tides. At high tide, water fills the harbour. At low tide, the harbour is empty, and the boats are stranded on the sand.

High tide

Low tide

**DID YOU KNOW?**

The Bay of Fundy in Canada has very high and very low tides. The water level changes by up to 16 metres.

143

# Rocky coasts

High cliffs tower above the sea on some coastlines. Other shores have wide, sandy bays, headlands or amazing rock arches. All of these landscapes are formed by the pounding waves.

## Steep cliffs

Waves crash onto the shore every minute of every day. Water, grit and pebbles smash against rocky coasts, chipping bits away. Steep cliffs form where hills meet the ocean.

## Headlands and bays

As waves beat against the shore, soft rocks wear away more quickly than hard rocks. The sea cuts deep, curving bays into soft rocks. Hard rocks stand up to the waves, forming headlands that stick far out to sea.

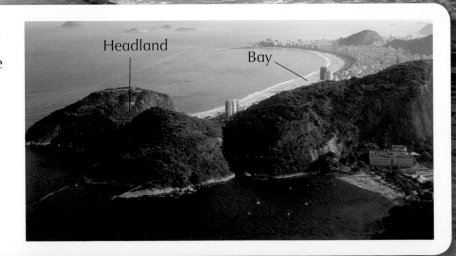

Headland

Bay

144

## Rock arch

Rock arches form where waves eat into a headland from both sides. This makes two caves, which eventually wear right through to make an arch. This arch is in the Galapagos Islands in South America.

Arch is worn by the waves.

Direction of waves

Arch collapses to leave a stack.

## How stacks form

Waves continue to crash against a rock arch. Eventually, the top of the arch crumbles, leaving a pillar of rock standing in the ocean. The pillar is called a stack.

145

# On the beach

Beaches can be sandy or pebbly. Most people prefer a sandy beach to any other kind of beach – and some animals do too!

## How do beaches form?

Rivers carry sand and rocks out to sea. Waves also chip pieces off cliffs. Beaches form where waves dump the sand and rocks in sheltered bays.

A sandy beach has formed in this bay in Cornwall, UK.

## Sandy or pebbly

Sand is made of tiny bits of rock or shell. Rivers and waves have smashed the rocks and shells into tiny pieces. Pebbles on beaches are small rocks that have been worn smooth by the water.

# Beach wildlife

All sorts of animals live on beaches. Crabs, worms and cockles burrow into the sand. Gulls search for fish by the water's edge. Shellfish, such as limpets, cling to the rocks.

Crabs have large claws, which they use to grab food.

## Shifting sideways

Where waves strike the shore at an angle, they shift sand and pebbles sideways. This material can pile up out to sea to make a strip of land called a spit. Groynes are fences built across a beach to stop the sand moving along the beach.

Spit

Direction of waves

Groyne

# Islands

Islands are areas of land completely surrounded by water. Some islands, such as Britain, are big, but many islands are small. There are islands in rivers and lakes, as well as in the sea.

## Volcanic islands

Islands that lie far out to sea are often the tips of underwater volcanoes. The volcano erupts on the seabed and lava builds up to make a mountain. The mountain eventually breaks the water's surface, forming an island.

## Near the mainland

Some islands lie close to large land masses called continents. Britain was once joined to mainland Europe but became an island when the sea level rose thousands of years ago.

Ireland

Britain

Europe

A volcanic island in Alaska, USA.

A ring of coral

## Coral islands

This island is made of a hard material called coral (see pages 150–151). Sometimes a ring of coral forms around a small volcanic island. The island may later sink due to the movement of the Earth's crust, leaving just the coral.

## Island life

Many remote islands are home to animals found nowhere else. The giant tortoise lives on a group of islands called the Galapagos Islands in South America.

# Great Barrier Reef

Coral reefs form in warm, shallow seas. They aren't made of rock, but are built from small creatures called coral polyps. The Great Barrier Reef, off Australia, is the world's largest coral reef.

## Coral homes

Coral reefs are hard ridges just below the surface of the sea. They are home to many ocean creatures including brightly coloured fish, shrimps and starfish. Turtles and sharks swim nearby.

## Barrier Reef facts

- The Great Barrier Reef is made up of 2500 smaller reefs. The reef stretches for 2000 kilometres, and is so large that it can be seen from space.
- More than 1500 different types of fish live on the Great Barrier Reef.

# Reef builders

A coral polyp has a chalky body and arm-like tentacles. When a polyp dies, its chalky body remains. Millions of bodies build up on top of one another to form a coral reef.

Coral tentacles

## Reef stingers

Sea anemones live on the reef. The stings of these animals kill most fish, but clownfish are safe because their bodies are protected by a special slime.

## Scary sharks

Sharks hunt in the clear waters by the reef. These big fish have a very good sense of smell. When they smell the blood of a wounded creature, they swim up for the kill.

### DID YOU KNOW?

Coral only grows a few centimetres a year. It takes millions of years for a large reef to form.

The pointed fin sticks out of the water when a shark swims near the surface.

Jellyfish

Sunlit zone:
0–200 metres

Mackerel

Mid-depths:
200–2000
metres

Sperm
whale

Giant squid

Deep sea:
2000–4000
metres

Gulper eel

Anglerfish

Depths below
4000 metres
are called
the abyss.

# Open ocean

In the open ocean, water stretches out on all sides and for several kilometres downwards. The water can be divided into layers, with different creatures living at different depths.

## Ocean layers

The upper waters are lit by the sunlight. Jellyfish and mackerel swim there. Sperm whales and giant squid swim in the dim mid-waters. Gulper eels and anglerfish live in the inky-black depths.

## Plankton

Tiny plants and animals called plankton float on the ocean surface. These creatures are so small you can only see them using a microscope. Plankton provide food for many larger creatures, including whales.

## At the surface

Large, powerful fish called marlin chase after the shoals of mackerel on the surface. They snap up the small fish with their long, pointed snouts.

## Diving to the depths

Sperm whales come to the surface to breathe. Then they dive to depths of 1000 metres to hunt giant squid. Many sperm whales are scarred by battles with squid.

Marlin can swim at speeds of up to 80 kilometres an hour.

### DID YOU KNOW?

The ocean's deepest point is the Marianas Trench in the western Pacific. It lies 10,920 metres below the surface. In 1961, two scientists went to the bottom in a submarine.

# On the seabed

Many creatures live on the seabed. Starfish and flatfish live in fairly shallow water. Other creatures lurk on the bed of the deep oceans, where there are mountains, cliffs and volcanoes similar to those on land.

## Flatfish

Flatfish rest on the seabed. The speckled colours of this plaice blend in with the sand. The fish changes colour when it moves on to rock or weeds, allowing it to hide from its enemies.

## Ocean floor

Long mountain chains run down the centre of the oceans. The flat plains on either side may be dotted with volcanoes or cut by deep trenches. The seabed slopes upwards to broad, flat shelves that edge the land.

Sea level

Seamounts (remains of dead volcanoes)

Mountain chain called a mid-ocean ridge

Broad ledge (continental shelf)

Steep slope

Plain

## Starfish

Starfish creep along the seabed. Most starfish have five arms, but some have up to 20. A starfish can regrow an arm if it gets bitten off by an enemy.

Plain

Deep trench

## Mapping the seabed

Scientists map the seabed using a technique called sonar. They aim sound waves at the bottom and listen to the echoes that bounce back. The time taken by the echoes tells them how deep it is.

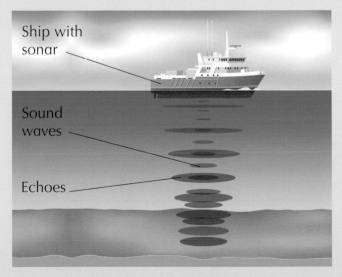

Ship with sonar

Sound waves

Echoes

# The deep sea

The deep sea is the last unexplored place on the Earth because it is so difficult to get to. Only a few submarines can descend that deep.

## Deep sea submarine

This special submarine can explore the bottom of the ocean. It is called *Alvin* and carries three people. *Alvin* has two arms that can collect samples.

## Black smokers

In 1977, scientists exploring a deep sea ridge made an amazing discovery. They found strange chimneys spouting clouds of black, boiling-hot water. These undersea volcanoes are called black smokers.

Viperfish

Anglerfish

Brittlestar

## Fish of the deep

Deep sea fish hunt in the cold, black water. Many have huge mouths and stretchy stomachs so they can swallow any prey they find. Some can swallow prey twice their own size!

## Life at black smokers

Strange creatures live around the black smokers. There are blind crabs, eyeless shrimps and long, slim tube worms. The hot water, rich in minerals, helps these creatures to stay alive.

**DID YOU KNOW?** Deep-sea fish are built to stand the enormous pressure caused by the weight of all the water pressing down from above. Deep sea fish can explode if brought to the surface!

A crab near a black smoker.

# Icy seas

The seas in the polar regions are covered with ice for much of the year. There are towering icebergs and huge, flat-topped ice shelves. When the sea freezes over, a different type of ice – pack ice – forms.

## Ice shelf

Huge ice shelves edge the land in the polar regions. They form where glaciers meet the ocean, and the ice breaks off and floats out to sea.

A thick coat of feathers keeps out the cold.

## Penguins

Penguins live on the coasts of Antarctica. They walk with a waddle on land, but are fast swimmers. They dive into the icy water to hunt fish. Penguins cannot fly, but they flap their wings to swim under water.

Sea level

Four-fifths of an iceberg lies below the surface.

# Icebergs

Icebergs form when a large chunk of ice breaks off an ice shelf or a glacier. Icebergs can be a danger to ships. Only a small part of an iceberg shows above the surface – the rest is below.

**DID YOU KNOW?**

The biggest iceberg ever seen had a surface area the size of Belgium! Icebergs can also be up to 150 metres high.

## Sinking of the Titanic

In 1912, a luxury passenger ship called the *Titanic* hit an iceberg in the North Atlantic Ocean. The ship sank in just four hours, and 1500 people drowned. The *Titanic's* owners had claimed it was unsinkable!

# Ocean treasures

All sorts of riches come from the ocean. As well as fish and shellfish, there are valuable minerals, such as oil and gas. Harvesting the ocean's riches, however, is often easier said than done!

## Fishing boats

Fishermen set traps and nets to catch fish and shellfish. Different nets are used to catch fish at the surface and on the bottom. Modern fishing boats catch so many fish that some fish are now rare.

## Pearls

Pearls are valuable gems made by shellfish called oysters. When a piece of grit gets inside an oyster's shell, a hard, shiny ball, called a pearl, forms around the grit. Diving deep for pearls can be dangerous.

A pearl diver collects oysters from baskets in Thailand.

# Oil and gas

Oil and gas are mined from the seabed in shallow waters. A platform called a rig may stand on stilts or may float, anchored to the bottom. Engineers drill into the seabed to reach the oil or gas, and then pump it to the surface.

## Salt

People get salt from the oceans by flooding shallow ponds near the sea with seawater. The water dries in the sun, leaving behind the salt.

This salt has been raked into piles.

NORTH CORMORANT

**DID YOU KNOW?** Many modern fishing boats have freezers on board. The fish are frozen soon after being caught to keep them fresh. This allows boats to stay out at sea longer.

### The kraken

Legends tell of a sea monster called the kraken. The tales said it would trap ships in its tentacles and drag them down to the seabed. Experts believe these stories were based on the giant squid.

# Mysteries of the ocean

The undersea world holds many mysteries and also dangers. In past times, stories of sea monsters helped to explain the dangers. We now understand a lot more about the oceans, but some mysteries remain.

### Rocky reefs

Rocks and sandbanks can be very dangerous for ships, especially in fog or storms. Lighthouses warn ships away from the rocks. In the past, lighthouse keepers controlled the lights, but now most lighthouses work automatically.

**DID YOU KNOW?**

In 1872, a ship called the *Mary Celeste* was found drifting in the Atlantic Ocean. The crew and passengers had all vanished. No one has fully explained this mystery.

## Myth of the mermaid

In days gone by, sailors reported seeing mermaids. These legendary creatures were said to look like women with a fish's tail. Experts believe the stories are based on sightings of real, seal-like creatures called dugongs.

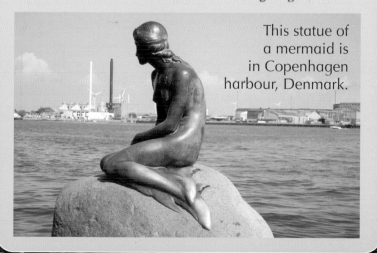

This statue of a mermaid is in Copenhagen harbour, Denmark.

## Diving for treasure

In dangerous waters, wrecks of sunken ships lie on the seabed. Some ships sank carrying gold, silver and jewels. Divers search the wrecks and sometimes bring treasure to the surface.

163

# Air and weather

Weather is created by the Sun heating the earth, which makes the air move around. This produces constantly changing conditions, from clear blue skies to gusting winds and deafening thunderstorms. This chapter will explain about air and weather. Find out how clouds form and why it rains. Discover how animals and people cope with different weather. Learn how experts can predict the weather.

# The atmosphere

The Earth is wrapped in a protective blanket of gases called the atmosphere. This blanket makes life possible on the Earth. Our weather is created in the lowest layer.

800 km

Atmosphere stretches about 800 km above the Earth's surface. Beyond is space.

500 km

80 km

Exosphere

Thermosphere

Mesosphere

Stratosphere

Troposphere

0 km

## Blanket of gases

The main atmosphere gases are nitrogen and also oxygen, which is vital for life. Small amounts of other gases help to trap the Sun's heat and filter out harmful rays. The Earth's gravity keeps the atmosphere in place.

## Layers of atmosphere

The atmosphere has five layers stacked on top of one another. The lowest, the troposphere, contains 75 per cent of the atmosphere's gases. The air thins out as you head towards the exosphere and space.

## Thin air

The higher you go, the less oxygen there is. Mountaineers use bottled oxygen in the 'thin air' to help them breathe. The air on the highest mountains contains about one third of the gases found at sea level.

## Above the clouds

Clouds form in the lowest layer of the atmosphere. Planes can climb to the next layer, the stratosphere, to get above the clouds and avoid storms.

Top of cloud cover

**DID YOU KNOW?**

The Earth's atmosphere helps to protect us from meteors – rocks falling from space. Meteors usually burn up high in the atmosphere, to form 'shooting stars'.

1% other gases

21% oxygen

78% nitrogen

# Air

The air in the atmosphere contains a mixture of gases. The constant recycling of these gases links the atmosphere to the living world of plants, animals and humans.

## What is air made of?

This balloon shows the amounts of gases that make up air. There is almost four times as much nitrogen as oxygen. The other gases include carbon dioxide and water vapour.

## Plant life

Trees and plants use carbon dioxide, water and sunlight to grow, in a process called photosynthesis. They give off oxygen as waste. Nitrogen in the soil helps to nourish plants.

## DID YOU KNOW?

The balance of gases in the atmosphere has remained the same for about a billion years.

# Animal life

Living creatures need oxygen to live. When we breathe in, oxygen passes from our lungs into our blood. Blood is pumped all around our body and provides the oxygen we need to live, move and grow. We breathe out carbon dioxide as waste.

Horses breathe in oxygen and breathe out carbon dioxide, just as we do.

## Breathing underwater

Fish also need oxygen to live. They take oxygen from water using feathery structures called gills. As water passes over the gills, they filter off the oxygen.

This slit leads to the fish's gills.

# Light as air

Air is light. However, the weight of all the air above presses down on you. This is known as air pressure. You can't feel the air pushing against you because the air inside you pushes back. But you can see its effects.

## Floating and falling

If you drop a ball and a feather, the ball reaches the ground first. Both are pulled by gravity, but the air pushes against the wispy feather more than the smooth, curved ball, so the ball falls faster.

## Blowing bubbles

When you blow soapy bubbles, warm air from your lungs fills the bubbles. Warm air is lighter than cold air so the bubbles drift upwards. They sink as the air inside cools.

## Hot-air balloon

A hot-air balloon climbs high in the sky because a burner heats the air inside the balloon. This makes the balloon lighter than the surrounding air, so the balloon rises.

## Rising air

When the sun heats a mass of air, the warm air starts to rise. This creates a current of warm, rising air called a thermal. Birds use thermals to glide for hours, hardly flapping their wings.

The gull's large wings help it glide on thermals.

Basket below the balloon carries people.

**DID YOU KNOW?** Hang gliders are like large kites that pilots hang from to fly through the air. They use thermals to rise high in the sky.

# Wind

Wind is moving air. The wind blows when the Sun heats the Earth's surface unevenly. Moving air brings different kinds of weather, such as clouds and rain.

## Why do winds blow?

Warm air weighs less than cold air and rises. Cooler air rushes in to fill the space left by the warm air. This movement of air is what makes the wind blow.

You need a strong wind to fly a kite!

## Wind speed

A wind's strength depends on its speed. A slow wind rustles leaves. A medium wind will make flags flutter. A very fast wind can sometimes uproot trees.

# Using the wind

People use the wind in many ways. Wind turns the sails of windmills. The moving sails turn a grindstone, which crushes wheat into flour. Wind also pushes on the sails of yachts, making them move across the sea.

Wooden sail

## Weather vanes

Weather vanes such as this one turn to show which way the wind is blowing. In most areas, the wind usually blows from one direction. This is called the prevailing wind.

### DID YOU KNOW?

Modern windmills called wind turbines use energy from the wind to make electricity. The sails turn generators which produce electricity.

173

# Cloudy skies

Clouds are masses of floating moisture.
They are made of millions of tiny water drops
or ice crystals. Clouds form when warm air
containing moisture rises and cools.

Cumulus clouds drift across
the sky in summer.

## Fluffy cumulus

If you watch the sky you will
see clouds of different shapes.
Different clouds bring different
types of weather. White, fluffy
clouds, known as cumulus,
usually mean fine weather.

174

Flat-topped
cumulonimbus
clouds

## Wispy cirrus

Cirrus clouds form very high in the sky. They are made from ice crystals. The wind sometimes blows these white clouds into wispy shapes, like horses' tails.

## Storm clouds

Cumulonimbus clouds are towering, flat-topped clouds. If you see these clouds, watch out for bad weather! They often bring heavy rain, hail or thunderstorms (see pages 202–203 and 210–211).

Thick, grey stratus
clouds

## Thick stratus

Stratus clouds are low-level clouds. Sometimes they cover the whole sky in a thick grey blanket. These clouds may bring drizzle, rain or snow.

### DID YOU KNOW?

Cirrus are the highest clouds. They usually form 6–12 kilometres up in the sky. Cumulonimbus clouds are very tall and can tower up to nine kilometres high.

# It's raining!

Sooner or later, clouds shed their moisture as rain, snow, sleet or hail. This is called precipitation. Very fine rain is called drizzle. A short burst of rain is called a shower.

## Rain from ice

In very high clouds, the moisture forms ice instead of water. Tiny ice crystals join up to make snowflakes. Snowflakes often melt on the way down to fall as rain.

## Rain storm

Tiny drops of water in clouds join together to make bigger drops. When the raindrops become too heavy they fall to the ground. A very heavy shower is called a cloudburst.

The sky turns grey when the clouds become thick.

## DID YOU KNOW?

Raindrops are not shaped like teardrops. They are round with a flatter top and bottom, like hamburger buns.

## Rainbows

If the sun comes out when it's raining, you may see a rainbow. Raindrops bend the different colours in white light, separating them out into red, orange, yellow, green, blue, indigo and violet.

## Keeping dry

A raincoat and rubber boots will keep you dry in wet weather. An umbrella will keep you extra dry! They are all made of waterproof materials that keep out the rain.

# The water cycle

Moisture moves between the air, oceans and land in a never-ending cycle. As the water moves around, it changes from a liquid into a gas and back again.

## Powered by the Sun

The Sun powers the water cycle by warming the air. Warm air holds more moisture than cold air. When warm, moist air cools, clouds form and bring rain.

Sun

**2.** Warm, moist air blows inland.

**1.** Moisture rises into the air.

**5.** Rivers drain into the sea.

## Rising moisture

As the Sun warms the sea, moisture rises into the air in the form of a gas called water vapour. This process is known as evaporation. Winds blow the warm, moist air towards the land.

**3.** Clouds form as warm air rises and cools.

**4.** Rain falls from clouds and runs into rivers.

## Clouds form

When warm, moist air rises over hills or mountains, it cools. The water vapour turns into tiny drops of water or ice, which gather to make clouds. The clouds bring rain, snow or hail.

## DID YOU KNOW?

The rain that falls where you live has fallen many times before in other places. No new water forms on the Earth – it is just recycled naturally.

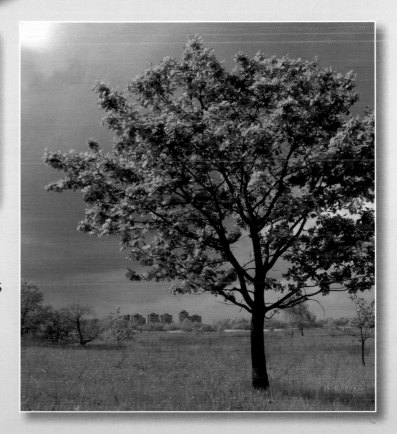

## Soaking up water

When it rains, some water drains into rivers and travels back to the sea. Rainwater also soaks into the ground. Trees draw up moisture through their roots and release it through their leaves.

## Dew

Dew forms on thin, cold surfaces in the morning or evening. As the surface cools, moisture from the air collects on it. When it's very cold, the dew becomes frost.

Water appears on leaves as dew drops or frost.

# Dew, mist and fog

Dew, mist and fog all form when moisture in the air collects into water droplets. This happens when the air cools suddenly, for example, when it blows over a cold surface.

## Mist

Mist is low cloud that touches the Earth's surface. Mountains are often misty because the air is colder there.

Llamas roaming in the misty Andes Mountains in Peru.

## Fog

Fog is thick mist, where you can see less than one kilometre ahead. Fog can be dangerous. Drivers have to use bright fog lights and take extra care when driving.

## Smog

Smog is a dirty haze of smoke and fog that hangs over cities. It forms in air that has been polluted by fumes from cars and factories. People who live in smoggy cities can have trouble breathing.

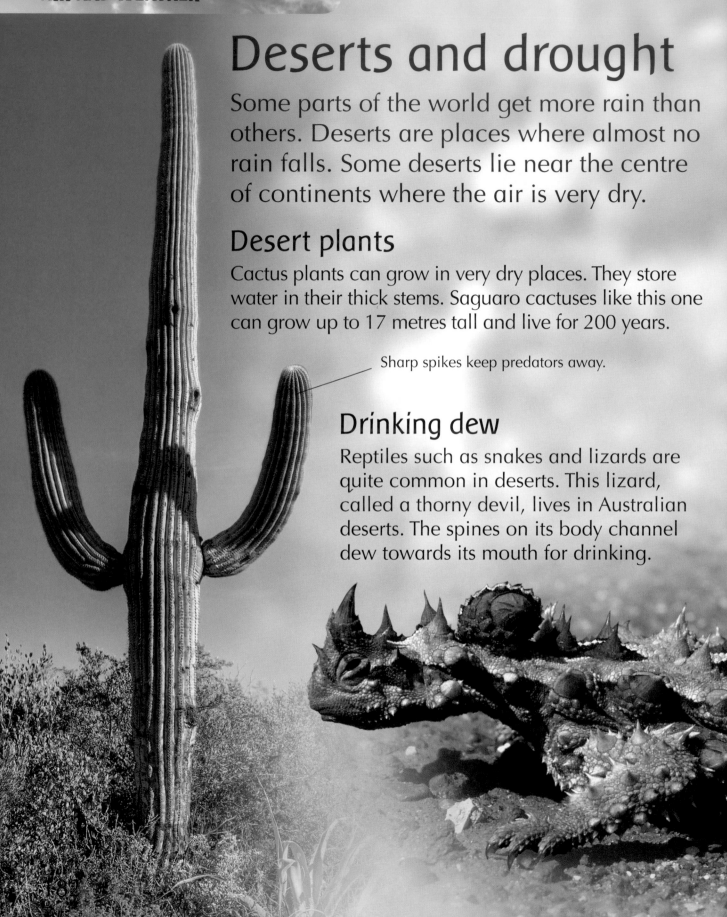

# Deserts and drought

Some parts of the world get more rain than others. Deserts are places where almost no rain falls. Some deserts lie near the centre of continents where the air is very dry.

## Desert plants

Cactus plants can grow in very dry places. They store water in their thick stems. Saguaro cactuses like this one can grow up to 17 metres tall and live for 200 years.

Sharp spikes keep predators away.

## Drinking dew

Reptiles such as snakes and lizards are quite common in deserts. This lizard, called a thorny devil, lives in Australian deserts. The spines on its body channel dew towards its mouth for drinking.

## Desert in bloom

When rain finally falls in the desert, seeds sprout and plants bloom quickly. For a few days, the desert becomes a carpet of flowers. But the flowers soon wither as dry weather returns.

## Drought

A drought is a long time without rain. Some parts of Africa are regularly hit by drought. Crops and animals can die of thirst. People may have to move somewhere else until it rains.

Spines also protect the lizard from enemies.

### DID YOU KNOW?

The Atacama Desert in South America is the driest place on the Earth. Some parts have had no rain for centuries. The Andes Mountains shield this region from the wet ocean winds.

# The Sahara Desert

The Sahara Desert, which stretches across North Africa, is the world's largest desert. Plants, animals and people have to be survival experts to live in this harsh place.

EUROPE

ASIA

Sahara Desert

AFRICA

Red Sea

Atlantic Ocean

## World's biggest desert

This map shows the size of the Sahara. It stretches from the Red Sea to the Atlantic Ocean. The Sahara is actually getting bigger, as farmlands on the edge are hit by drought.

## Sand dunes

About a fifth of the Sahara is covered in sand. The rest is covered in stones. The wind blows the sand into high hills called dunes. Saharan sand dunes look red at sunset.

## Sahara facts

- The Sahara covers an amazing nine million sq km – an area the size of the United States.

- About 6000 years ago, the Sahara was much wetter. Cave paintings show that elephants and giraffes once lived in areas that are now desert.

- The tallest dunes in the Sahara are 465 metres high.

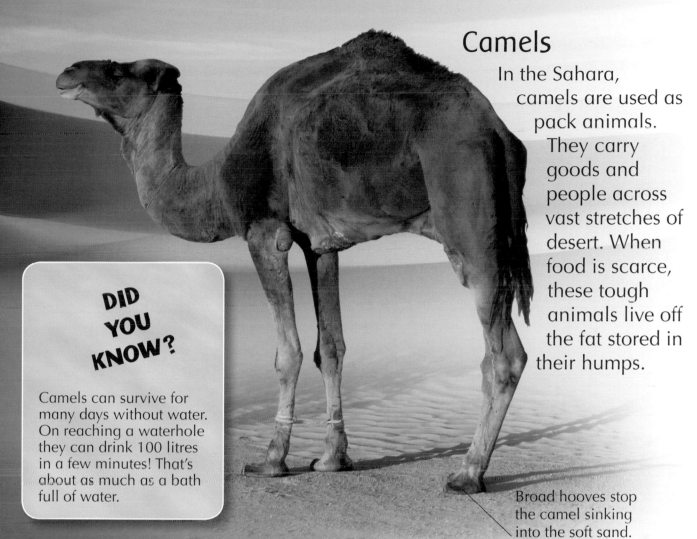

# Camels

In the Sahara, camels are used as pack animals. They carry goods and people across vast stretches of desert. When food is scarce, these tough animals live off the fat stored in their humps.

Broad hooves stop the camel sinking into the soft sand.

# Desert people

Some people in the Sahara are nomads. They wander from camp to camp, sleeping in tents and leading their camels in search of food and water. Today, many desert nomads have settled down to live in towns.

# Living with the weather

Furry hood and fleece jacket keep out icy winds.

All over the world, people have learned to cope with local weather conditions. The right clothes and the right type of home can keep people comfortable in scorching heat, bitter cold or heavy rain.

## Dressed for the cold

Some parts of the world have harsh winters with months of snow and ice. People dress in warm clothing when they go outside. Homes are cosy and well-heated.

Stilt houses have steep roofs that let the rain run off easily.

## Ready for floods

In regions that get heavy rain, flooding is common. In parts of Asia, some homes are built on stilts to keep them dry during floods. Small boats are used to travel about.

## Cave homes

In deserts and other places near the equator, the fierce heat can make life very uncomfortable. In parts of Africa and Australia, people keep cool in homes dug out of rock.

A hibernating groundhog.

## Hibernating animals

Animals have their own ways of dealing with harsh weather. Mammals such as this groundhog spend the winter months in a deep sleep called hibernation. Sleeping saves energy when food is scarce.

# Watching the weather

Weather plays a big part in our lives. It affects how we dress and whether we plan to be inside or outside. Knowing about the weather is especially important to farmers, sailors and anyone who works outdoors.

Weather balloons send information by radio.

## Weather balloon

Weather balloons measure conditions high in the atmosphere. They rise because they are filled with a light gas called helium. Aircraft and satellites also make records and watch out for storms.

## Weather stations

Weather stations all over the world measure rainfall, wind direction and speed, and air temperature – how warm or cold it is. These records are fed into computers, which help to work out what the weather will do next.

## Weather forecasts

Weather forecasters tell us what the weather will be like over the next day or so. They use symbols on maps to show the likely conditions, such as temperature, wind, sunshine and rain.

Key

Sun

Cloud

Rain

20 Temperature

5 Wind

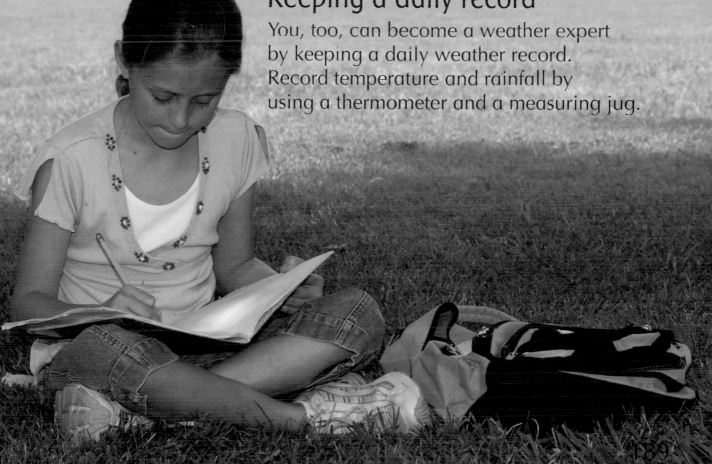

## Keeping a daily record

You, too, can become a weather expert by keeping a daily weather record. Record temperature and rainfall by using a thermometer and a measuring jug.

# Wild weather

Most places on the Earth are sometimes hit by severe weather, such as hurricanes, tornadoes, thunderstorms, hail and heavy snow. This chapter explains the causes of wild weather – including how hurricanes form and why stormclouds produce hail or lightning. Experts say the world's weather is getting warmer and wilder. Read on to find out why and how we can take care of the Earth.

# Hurricanes

Huge spinning storms with powerful winds are called hurricanes. The winds whirl about a calm 'eye' in the centre. Hurricanes form over warm oceans and do a lot of damage when they hit land.

## How do hurricanes form?

As the Sun heats the ocean, warm, moist air rises to form thunderclouds. Cold air rushes in at the bottom. The thunderclouds merge and start to spin.

The inside of a hurricane

Air spirals around the eye and cools.

Warm, moist air rising

Eye

Direction of spin of hurricane

Strongest winds are around the eye.

Eye

## Whirling clouds

This picture of a hurricane was taken from space. It shows bands of cloud swirling around the eye in the centre. Hurricanes are enormous – they can measure 500 to 800 kilometres across.

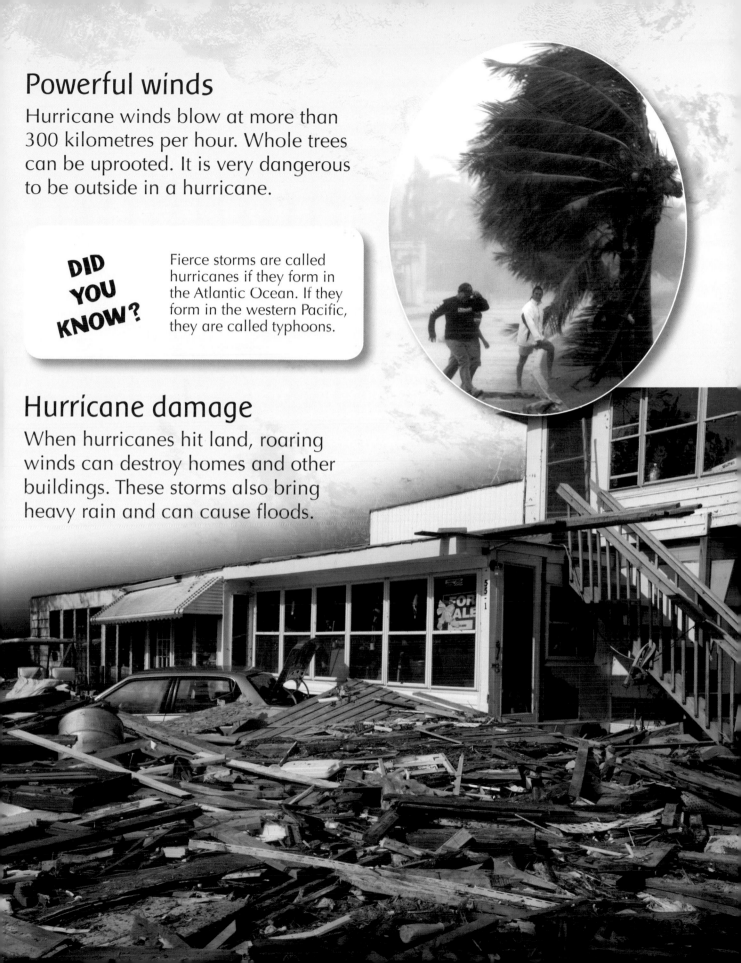

# Powerful winds

Hurricane winds blow at more than 300 kilometres per hour. Whole trees can be uprooted. It is very dangerous to be outside in a hurricane.

**DID YOU KNOW?**

Fierce storms are called hurricanes if they form in the Atlantic Ocean. If they form in the western Pacific, they are called typhoons.

# Hurricane damage

When hurricanes hit land, roaring winds can destroy homes and other buildings. These storms also bring heavy rain and can cause floods.

# Hurricane Katrina

In 2005, a powerful hurricane called Hurricane Katrina struck the southern United States. The coastal city of New Orleans was badly flooded. It was the most destructive storm that has ever hit the United States.

## Rising waters

Roaring winds, rough seas and heavy rain caused flooding. The Mississippi River spilled over high banks called levees that had been built to prevent flooding. Water poured into the nearby city of New Orleans.

## Wrecked towns

Hurricane Katrina wrecked seaside towns when it blew in off the ocean. Powerful winds tossed this truck into a tree. Boats were sucked out of the sea and hurled onto the shore.

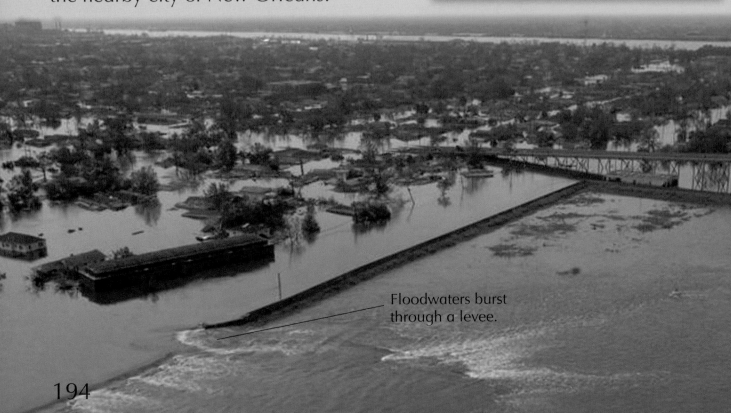

Floodwaters burst through a levee.

## Katrina facts

- Winds of up to 280 kilometres per hour were recorded during Hurricane Katrina.

- Floodwater covered four-fifths of New Orleans. Homes, shops and parks were covered by up to six metres of water.

## Boat rescue

City leaders ordered everyone to leave New Orleans. Helicopters and boats rescued people who had been stranded in their homes by the rising floodwater.

**DID YOU KNOW?** More than 1000 people died during Hurricane Katrina. About one million homes were damaged by the high winds and flooding.

## Returning home

When the water finally drained away, the levees were rebuilt. Damaged buildings then had to be repaired. It was a long time before it was safe for people to return to their homes. This family moved back a year later.

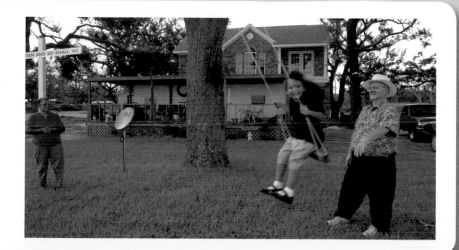

# Tornadoes

Tornadoes are small but very violent storms. A whirling funnel of air weaves across the landscape, sucking up debris. Tornadoes form on land, not out at sea.

Twisting funnel can tower up to 200 metres high.

Air descending from cloud

Spinning funnel of air

Eye

### Inside a tornado

Tornadoes are much smaller than hurricanes – usually less than one kilometre across – but the winds inside whirl even faster. As in a hurricane, the winds spiral around a calm central 'eye'.

## Touch down!

In hot, sticky weather, warm, moist air shoots upwards to form towering thunderclouds. A funnel of whirling air appears below the cloud. It forms a tornado when it touches the ground.

# Hit by a tornado

The superstrong winds of a tornado have tremendous power. But the path of destruction is usually narrow. A tornado may completely wreck one house but leave the next one untouched.

The damage caused by a tornado in Florida, USA, in 2007.

## DID YOU KNOW?

Winds of about 600 kilometres per hour have been recorded inside tornadoes. These are the fastest winds on the Earth.

The tornado does a lot of damage where it touches the ground.

## Tornado Alley

Tornadoes are most common in the United States. Each year, about 1000 tornadoes strike there. Most form in an area called Tornado Alley (coloured yellow on this map of the United States).

Tornado Alley

Gulf of Mexico

CANADA

New York

Michigan

Ohio

Indiana

West
Virginia

Illinois

Virginia

UNITED
STATES OF
AMERICA

Kentucky

North Carolina

Tennessee

Mississippi

Alabama

Georgia

# Tornado damage

Tornadoes travel only a short distance before dying out. But they leave a trail of destruction. Sometimes a whole group of tornadoes forms at once. This is called a tornado outbreak.

## Tornado outbreak

In 1974, a total of 148 tornadoes formed in a single day. The funnels swept across 13 US states, as shown on the map. They killed 330 people and left a path of devastation 4000 kilometres long!

## Tornado shelters

When a tornado strikes, the safest place to be is underground. Many homes in the USA have underground shelters in basements and cellars. People hide if they are told a tornado is due and come out when the danger has passed.

## Freak damage

The funnel of a tornado acts like a giant vacuum cleaner. It can suck roofs off houses and flatten buildings. It can pick up cars like toys and toss them into the air.

## Storm chasers

Most people will do anything to avoid a tornado. But experts called storm chasers enjoy watching tornadoes up close. When a tornado is reported, they race to the scene to photograph the storm.

# Freak storms

Hurricanes and tornadoes are not the only spinning storms. Whirlwinds can form over the sea or whip up sand in deserts. These storms are usually small but scary.

Cloud of sand picked up by a dust devil.

## Dust devils

Small tornadoes that form in deserts are called dust devils. The swirling air picks up sand and carries it up to 30 metres in the air. Despite their name, dust devils don't usually do much harm.

## Waterspouts

When a tornado strikes at sea, it forms a waterspout. The narrow, twisting funnel sucks up water and sometimes fish too. If the waterspout moves on to the land, it may dump a shower of fish!

Funnel of whirling clouds hits the sea.

## Shower of frogs!

Over the centuries, there have been many reports of animals or strange objects dropped by whirlwinds. In 1939, a shower of little frogs fell on a town in western England. Swirling winds had sucked the young frogs out of ponds.

## Sandstorms

High winds can whip up sandstorms in deserts. Stinging sand fills the air, and people run for shelter. Wind can carry sand for thousands of kilometres and then dump it far away.

### DID YOU KNOW?

In 1940, a shower of silver coins fell on the Russian town of Gorky. A whirlwind had carried off a hidden treasure chest, which then burst open, scattering coins.

A sandstorm in Pakistan has turned the sky orange.

# Thunderstorms

About 2000 thunderstorms rage somewhere on the Earth every minute. These storms can cause terrible damage. They usually happen in hot weather, when warm, moist air rises to form thunderclouds.

## What is lightning?

Swirling air in thunderclouds makes raindrops rub together. This produces tiny electric charges. Positive charges build up at the top of the cloud, negative charges build up at the bottom. Lightning sparks between the two.

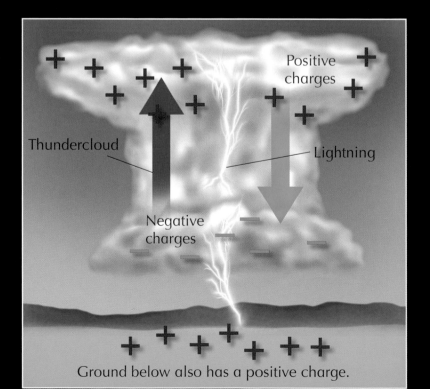

Positive charges

Thundercloud

Lightning

Negative charges

Ground below also has a positive charge.

## Static electricity

The type of electricity that builds up inside thunderclouds is called static electricity. This is the same kind of electricity that makes your hair stand on end if you brush it hard!

## Thunder clap

As lightning streaks through the sky, it heats the air to incredibly hot temperatures. The air explodes, causing a deafening crack of thunder. Light travels faster than sound, so you see the lightning before you hear the thunder.

**DID YOU KNOW?**

The sound of thunder takes three seconds to travel one kilometre. You can tell how far away a storm is by counting the seconds between the lightning and thunder and dividing the number by three.

## Forest fires

Lightning can start forest fires, especially in dry weather. In 1988, fires caused by lightning raged through Yellowstone National Park in the United States. Many thousands of acres of forest were burned.

# Streaks of lightning

Lightning is a huge spark of electricity. It can take different forms, depending on whether the spark flashes between clouds in the sky or shoots from a cloud to the ground below.

## Sheet lightning

When lightning flashes between clouds, it produces sheet lightning. The sparks light up the clouds from inside, so they glow (as above).

## Forked lightning

When lightning leaping downwards splits into many branches, it is called forked lightning. Lightning flashes downwards because the ground below has developed a positive charge.

Forked lightning hits a town in Utah, USA.

## DID YOU KNOW?

Being hit by lightning can be deadly. But some people survive, including champion golfer Lee Trevino, who was struck during a game.

## Lightning strike

Lightning always takes the fastest route to the ground. Sparks are attracted to tall objects, such as trees and high buildings. For this reason, people should never shelter under a tree in a storm.

Lightning hits the lightning rod on a tall building in Shanghai, China.

## Lightning rods

Tall buildings are often struck by lightning. A lightning rod makes the building safer. Lighting strikes the rod and then runs safely down a wire into the ground.

# Monsoon and floods

In some parts of the world, winds called monsoons change direction in different seasons. Summer monsoons bring heavy rain, which can cause flooding.

## Summer rain

Farmers rely on the monsoons to water their crops in summer. These farmers in India are planting rice during the monsoon rains.

## Changing winds

This diagram shows how monsoon rains in Asia change direction. In winter, winds blowing south from the mainland bring dry weather. In summer, winds blowing north off the ocean bring heavy rain.

Pakistan

India

Bangladesh

Indian Ocean

Key
Winter
Summer

## Hit by floods

Monsoon rains often cause floods in Bangladesh, a low-lying country next to India. Water flooded this village in Bangladesh after a heavy monsoon in 2007.

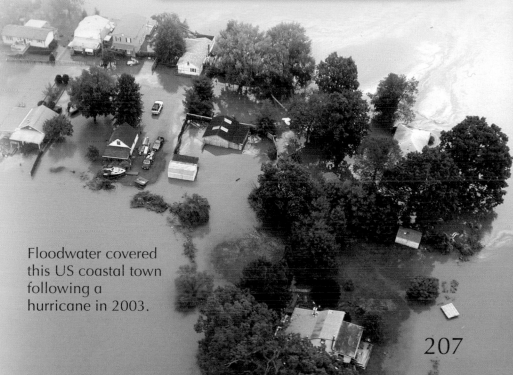

## Storm surges

As a hurricane moves over the sea, it sucks up water. The mound of water, called a storm surge, causes flooding when it hits the coast.

Floodwater covered this US coastal town following a hurricane in 2003.

# Snow and frost

In many parts of the world, winter brings frost, ice and snow. If you wrap up warm, this wild weather can be a lot of fun!

## Snow

Snow forms in clouds where the air is below freezing. The moisture in the clouds turns into ice crystals, which join to make snowflakes.

## Snowflakes

All snowflakes have six points or six sides. No two flakes are the same shape. A scientist studied snowflakes for 50 years without ever finding two that were exactly alike!

Snow is good for going sledging.

## Frost

In freezing weather, ice crystals form on leaves, windows and other cold surfaces. We call these crystals frost. Thick frost can look like a coating of snow.

## Icicles

Icicles may hang from roofs, trees and cliffs in cold weather. They form when water starts to drip and then freezes. As more water trickles down and freezes, the icicles grow longer and longer.

**DID YOU KNOW?**

Paradise in Mount Rainier National Park, USA, is one of the world's snowiest places. One year, 32 metres of snow fell on Paradise.

# Hail and blizzards

Extreme winter weather can be dangerous. When heavy snow combines with strong winds, we call it a blizzard. Hail is when pellets of ice fall from the clouds.

Drivers cannot see far in a blizzard, which makes driving dangerous.

## Snow storms

Swirling snow fills the air during a blizzard, and a layer of ice makes roads slippery. Roads can be blocked by the heavy snow.

The plough blade pushes the snow out of the way.

## How hail forms

Hailstones form when winds toss ice crystals up and down inside cold clouds. As the ice crystals rise and fall, more layers of ice are added, forming pellets of ice called hailstones. These hailstones eventually get so heavy they fall to the ground.

Hailstones are tossed up and down inside the cloud.

Heavy hailstones fall to the ground.

**DID YOU KNOW?**
The largest hailstone ever recorded fell on Aurora in central USA in 2003. The giant lump of ice measured 17 centimetres across.

Most hailstones are about the size of a pea, but some can be much bigger.

## Hail damage

Large hailstones do a lot of damage. Hailstones the size of baseballs can dent car roofs and smash windscreens. They can also flatten crops.

## Clearing snow

This snowplough is clearing a snowy road. Snow piles up on rooftops and branches during a blizzard. Trees, roofs and even power lines can collapse under the weight of snow.

# Changing weather

In recent years, wild weather has become much more common. Experts say that this is because the world is getting warmer and that harmful waste called pollution is to blame.

## Global warming

Power stations burn coal, oil and gas to provide energy. But they also release waste gases into the air. These gases are making the Earth heat up – this is called global warming.

## Greenhouse gases

Gases in the atmosphere trap some of the Sun's heat. They act like the glass in a greenhouse, so they are called greenhouse gases. Pollution is adding more of these gases into the air and this is making the Earth heat up.

Sun

Some of the Sun's heat is trapped by gases in the atmosphere.

Atmosphere

Earth

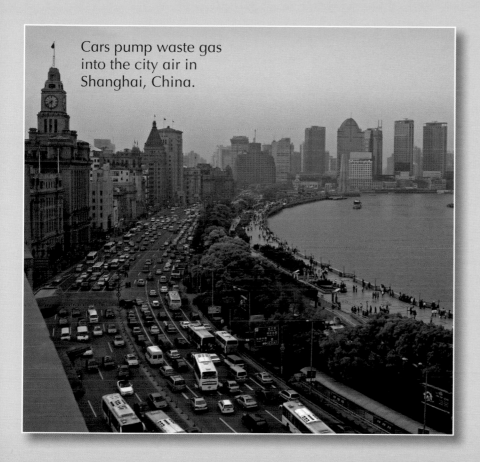

Cars pump waste gas into the city air in Shanghai, China.

## City pollution

Cars give off greenhouse gases. The air in cities is polluted by fumes from cars and factories. Cities cause a lot of pollution because so many people live there.

### DID YOU KNOW?

Temperatures rose by 0.5 degrees Celsius during the 20th century. Experts believe the Earth may start to heat up more quickly if we don't reduce pollution now.

## Melting ice sheets

Global warming is melting the ice in the polar regions. Melted ice is adding to the water in the oceans, making sea levels rise. This polar bear will have nowhere to hunt if all the ice melts.

Waves could flood this island in the Indian Ocean if sea levels rise.

# Caring for our Earth

Global warming is making sea levels rise. It is also causing more wild weather. We need to find ways of reducing the pollution that is making the Earth heat up.

## Rising seas

If sea levels carry on rising, cities by the coast could flood. Beautiful islands like this could disappear altogether. We need to produce less pollution to stop this happening.

## Cycling

Car journeys cause a lot of pollution. We can produce far less pollution by choosing different ways to travel. People should try to walk, cycle or take the train or bus to work or school.

## Recycling

Waste paper, glass, metal and plastic can be collected and sent to factories to be made into new materials. This is called recycling and helps to save energy.

A box of waste ready to be recycled.

## Saving energy

Power stations that provide us with electricity are adding to global warming. We can help by using energy more carefully. People should switch off lights, TVs and computers when they are not using them.

**DID YOU KNOW?**

Energy from the wind, Sun and flowing water can be used to make electricity without causing pollution. These forms of energy are kind to the Earth.

# Some useful words

### Air pressure
The weight of all the air pressing down on the Earth.

### Atmosphere
The layer of gases that surrounds the Earth.

### Aurora
Shimmering lights seen in the night sky at the North and South Poles.

### Axis
An imaginary line between the North and South Poles. The Earth rotates on its axis.

### Biome
A large area of the Earth's surface with a particular climate where similar types of plants grow.

### Cell
One of the tiny units of which living things are made up.

### Climate
The regular pattern of weather in an area.

### Crater
A hollow in the ground or in the top of a volcano.

### Crust
The Earth's hard outer layer.

### Crystal
A mineral with flat, smooth sides and a regular shape.

### Delta
A flat area at a river's mouth made of sand or mud dropped by the river.

### Drought
A period when no rain falls.

### Equator
An imaginary line around the centre of the Earth.

### Erosion
The wearing away of rocks by the weather.

### Eruption
When a volcano explodes ash and lava.

### Estuary
The part of a river's course where it nears the sea.

### Evacuation
When everyone has to leave an area to avoid danger.

216

## Fault
A crack in the Earth's crust formed by rocks shifting under the ground.

## Fossil
The remains of an ancient living thing that has been preserved, usually as stone.

## Fossil fuel
A fuel, such as coal or oil, made from the remains of prehistoric plants or animals.

## Fuel
A substance that can be burned to give off heat and light.

## Geyser
A hot underground spring that shoots out steam and boiling water.

## Gills
The feathery parts on a fish's head, used for breathing underwater.

## Glacier
A huge mass of ice that slides slowly downhill.

## Gravity
The pulling force of the Earth, which makes things fall to the ground.

## Greenhouse effect
The warming effect produced by gases in the air that trap the Sun's heat.

## Hemisphere
One half of the Earth, as divided by the equator.

## Humus
A layer on top of soil, made up of rotting plants.

## Hurricane
A huge spinning storm with very strong winds.

## Hydroelectric station
A place where electricity is made using energy from flowing water.

## Ice Age
A period in the past when the Earth's climate was much colder than it is today.

## Lava
Magma that bursts out when a volcano erupts.

## Levee
A high bank built along a river to prevent flooding.

## Magma
Red-hot rock deep beneath the Earth's crust.

## Magnet
A special piece of iron or steel that pulls iron and steel towards it.

## Magnetic field
The area around a magnet that is affected by the magnet's pull.

## Mantle
The thick layer inside the Earth below the crust, where the rocks are red-hot.

## Meander
A bend or loop in a river.

## Metal
A material, such as copper or gold, that is often shiny and can usually be shaped.

## Mineral
A solid, natural material from which rocks are formed.

## Monsoon
Winds that bring rain in the summer months in southern Asia.

## North Pole
The most northerly point on the Earth.

## Oasis
A place in a desert where water is found.

## Orbit
The path taken by a planet as it circles the Sun, or by a moon as it circles a planet.

## Ore
A rock that contains a metal.

## Photosynthesis
The forces by which plants use carbon dioxide, water and sunlight to grow.

## Plankton
Tiny plants and animals that float in the ocean.

## Plate
One of the huge slabs of rock that make up the Earth's crust.

## Polar regions
The areas around the North and South poles.

## Pollution
Any solid, liquid or gas that harms nature.

## Recycling
When materials such as glass, metal or plastic are used again rather than being thrown away.

## Seismograph
A machine used to measure the strength of earthquakes.

## Smog
A dirty fog produced by pollution.

## Solar system
The Sun and all the planets and rocks that circle around it.

## South Pole
The most southerly point on the Earth.

## Spit
A long finger of land that sticks out into the sea.

## Stack
A rocky pillar that stands in the sea.

## Storm surge
A mound of water that forms in the ocean beneath a hurricane.

## Temperate
An area with a mild climate.

## Temperature
How hot or cold it is.

## Tentacle
A long, arm-like structure on an animal.

## Thermal
A current of warm, rising air.

## Tornado
A funnel of spinning air that forms beneath a thundercloud.

## Tropics
The region on either side of the equator where the climate is hot.

## Tsunami
A giant wave caused by an earthquake or volcano.

## Water vapour
Water in the form of a gas. When water is heated, it turns into water vapour. This is called evaporation.

# Index

## A

air 98, 165, 168–171
air pressure 170
algae 20
Alps 90, 99, 101, 105, 108
Amazon River 126–127
amber 23
ammonites 22
Andes 88, 123, 126
Angel Falls, Venezuela 119
animals 46, 56, 84, 165,
        169
    and climate 28, 31, 99, 187
    beach 147
    caves 131
    desert 182, 185
    early 21, 24–25
    islands 149
    mountain 99, 102, 105
    nocturnal 13
    ocean 139, 150–157
    polar 33, 158
    soil 58–59
    water 120, 122, 125, 127
Antarctica 33, 110, 158
arches, rock 47, 145
Arctic 33, 110
atmosphere 166–168, 188
auroras 32
autumn 15, 29
avalanches 101

## B

bacteria 20
Baikal, Lake 122

basalt 39
bats 131
beaches 146–147
Ben Nevis, Scotland 93
biomes 28–29, 31
birds 46, 99, 119, 120,
        124, 171
black smokers 156, 157
blizzards 210–211
boats 117, 123, 134–135,
        160, 161, 173, 186, 195
bridges 135
Bryce Canyon, USA 46–47
bubbles 170

## C

cactus 182
camels 185
canals 134
canyons 113, 116
carbon dioxide 168, 169
cars 213, 214
Caspian Sea 122
caves 113, 128, 130–131,
        145, 184, 187
chalk 43
chamois 99
cirrus clouds 175
cities 27, 82, 132, 213
clay 42, 57
cliffs 37, 43, 96–97, 144
climate 25, 26–33
climbing 94, 95
clothing 186, 188
clouds 19, 27, 165, 167
    formation 179
    hurricanes 192
    types 174–175
coal 35, 54, 212

coasts 26, 141, 144–147,
        214
cold climates 15, 27, 29,
        32–33, 88, 98
coldest place 33
compass 17
conglomerate 43
copper 49, 103
coral 139, 149, 150–151
crags 96–97
craters 19, 65, 123
crocodiles 125
crust, the Earth's 18, 19,
        36–37, 122
crystals 53
cumulus clouds 174
currents 139, 140

## D

dams 78, 133
Dartmoor 97
day 9, 12, 15
Dead Sea 141
deltas 124, 125, 126
deserts 28, 129, 182–185,
        187, 200
dew 180, 182
diamonds 35, 52, 53
dinosaurs 24, 25
drizzle 176
drought 183, 184
dust devils 200

## E

Earth 9–33
    forces 16–17
    formation 9, 18–19
    in solar system 10, 11
    layers 18, 19, 36–37, 122

movement 10, 12–15
 tilt 14–15, 30, 32
earthquakes 44, 61, 62, 63,
 76–85
electricity 54, 133, 202,
 204, 215
equator 11, 26, 30, 31
erosion 40–41, 46–47, 56
 coastal 144, 145
 glaciers 108–109
 mountains 93, 108–109
 rivers 115, 128
estuaries 124
Everest, Mount 89, 94–95
evolution 20

## F

factories, 132, 133, 213
farming 59, 102, 132, 206
faults 62, 92
fires 78, 203
fireworks 49
fish 21, 117, 127, 151,
 153, 154, 157, 169
fishing 160, 161
fjords 109
floodplains 114, 120
floods 127, 136, 186, 214
 hurricanes 193, 194–195
 monsoon 206–207
flowers 15, 98, 183
fog 181
forces 16–17, 46, 61
forests 29, 69, 203
fossil fuels 35, 54–55
fossils 22–23, 25, 43
frog showers 201
frost 35, 40, 180, 209
fuels 35, 54–55

## G

Galapagos Islands 149
gas 35, 55, 74, 161, 212
 atmosphere 166, 168
gemstones 52–53
geysers 73
Giant's Causeway 39
glaciers 106–109, 122
global warming 55, 212–215
gneiss 44
gold 35, 50, 51, 103
gorges 116
Grand Canyon 36, 116, 117
granite 39, 48, 97
grasslands 31
gravity 16, 17, 18, 143,
 166, 170
Great Barrier Reef 150–151
greenhouse gases 212
Gulf Stream 141

## H

hail 47, 175, 191, 211
herons 120
hibernation 99, 187
hiking 104
Himalayas 89, 90, 94, 103,
 116
hoodoos 46
hot climates 15, 28, 30–31
hot springs 72
hot-air balloons 171
hurricanes 191, 192–195, 207

## I J K

ice 27, 32, 33, 40, 46, 47
 glaciers 106–109
 sea ice 158–159

Ice Ages 111
ice caps 110–111, 213
icebergs 158, 159
icicles 209
Iguacú Falls 119
iron 17, 47, 51
islands 139, 148–149, 214
jewels 52–53
Kilimanjaro, Mount 89
Krakatoa 81

## L

lakes 109, 113, 121–123,
 135
landslides 40, 78, 79, 100
lava 38, 39, 64–67
life 9, 10, 20–21, 24–25,
 166, 168, 169
light, speed of 13
lighthouses 162
lightning 202, 204–205
limestone 40, 45, 46, 128
lizards 182
llamas 99

## M

magma 38, 39, 44, 64
magnetism 16, 17
mammoths 111
marble 45
Marianas Trench 153
meanders 121
mermaids 163
metals 50–51
meteorites 19, 25
meteors 167
minerals 47, 48–49, 57,
 102, 140, 160
mining 37, 49, 54, 103, 161

Mississippi River 136, 194
mist 180, 181
monsoon 206–207
Monument Valley, USA 96
Moon 13, 16, 143
mountains 37, 87–105, 155
   air 98, 167
   animals 99, 105
   climate 27, 30, 88, 98,
      180
   dangers 100–101
   erosion 96–97, 108–109
   formation 42, 90–93
   highest 89, 93, 94–95
   plants 98
   tourism 104–105
   types 90–93
   underwater 154, 155
   volcanic 64, 66–67, 91,
      148
mud 70, 71, 73, 78, 79,
     121

## N

New Orleans 194–195
Niagara Falls 118
night 9, 12–13, 15
Nile River 115, 125, 132
nitrogen 166, 168
nomads 185

## O

oases 129
oceans 11, 16, 19, 37, 139–
     163
   animals 20, 21, 24, 139,
     150–157
   deep sea 153, 156–157
   icy 158–159

   layers 152–153
   mysteries 162–162
   ocean floor 154–155
   volcanoes 66
Oetzi, the ice man 107
oil 35, 55, 161, 212
ores 50
oxbow lakes 121
oxygen 20, 166, 167, 168,
     169

## P

Pacific Ocean 140
pearls 160
pebbles 146, 147
penguins 33, 158
photosynthesis 168
piranhas 127
planets 10–11, 16, 18
plankton 152
plants 20, 25, 28, 56, 57,
     98, 168, 182
plaster casts 48
plates 62, 63, 90, 92
plesiosaurs 24
ploughing 59
polar bears 33, 213
poles 11, 14, 17, 26, 32,
     33, 110–111, 158, 213
pollution 55, 137, 181,
     212–214
potholing 130
power station 54, 212,
     215
precipitation 176
prehistory 24–25, 105, 131
pterosaurs 24
puddingstone 43
pumice 38

## R

rain 19, 27, 31, 165, 175,
     176–177, 179
   erosion 35, 40, 47
   monsoon 206–207
rainbows 177
rainforests 31
rapids 117
recycling 215
reefs 150–151, 162
reptiles 24, 182
rescue dogs 101
rivers 41, 42, 113, 114–127,
     140, 146, 179
   deltas 124, 125, 126
   longest 115
   safety 136–137
   underground 128–129
   using 132–135
   waterfalls 118–119
rocks 35–37, 91
   coasts 144–145
   erosion 35, 40–41, 46–
     47, 56, 96
   space rocks 18, 19, 25
   types 38–39, 42–45

## S

Sahara Desert 184–185
salmon 117
salt 140, 141, 161
San Francisco 78, 82, 85
sand 146–147, 184
sandstone 42, 43, 46
sandstorms 201
sea anemones 151
sea levels 213, 214
sea monsters 162

seas *see* oceans
seasons 9, 14, 30
seismograph 84
sharks 151
sherpas 95
showers 176
silver 35, 50, 103
slate 44
smog 181
snow 27, 30, 32, 47, 88, 191, 208, 210
snowflakes 176, 208
soil 35, 56–57, 72, 120, 168
  life in 58–59
solar system 10, 16, 18
sonar 155
spits 147
spring 15
St Helens, Mount 68–69, 75
stacks 145
stalactites 128, 130
stalagmites 128, 130
starfish 155
stars 11, 13
steel 51
storm surges 207
storms 47, 188, 200–201
  hurricanes 192–195
  thunderstorms 175, 202–203
  tornadoes 196–199
stratus clouds 175
stromatolites 20
submarines 156
sulphur 49
summer 14, 15, 32
Sun 10, 11, 16, 18, 19, 171, 178

sunlight 12, 13, 26, 32, 35, 40, 168
sunrise and sunset 12

T

Taj Mahal, India 45
tarns 109
temperate zones 29
terraces 102
Thames Barrier 137
thermals 171
thunderstorms 175, 202–203
tides 139, 142–143
*Titanic* 159
Titicaca, Lake 123
tornadoes 191, 196–200
tors 97
towns and villages 103, 132, 185
transport 105, 113, 123, 134, 214
treasure 163
trees 15, 29, 57, 98, 168, 179
trilobites 21
tropics 26, 30
tsunamis 80
tundra 29
typhoons 193

U V

Uluru, Australia 97
valleys 92, 108, 114, 120–121
Vesuvius, Mount 70
volcanoes 19, 61, 62–74, 91, 154
  eruptions 64–65, 68–71, 81

lava 38, 39, 64–67
  studying 74–75
  types 66–67
  undersea 66, 154, 156
volcanic islands 148

W Y

water 35, 40, 46, 115, 129, 132
water cycle 178–179
water pressure 157
water vapour 168, 178
waterfalls 118–119
waterspouts 200
waves 139, 142, 147
weather 26, 98, 165, 166, 172–189
  severe 191–211
weather balloons 188
weather forecasts 189
weather stations 188
weather vanes 173
wells 129
whales 152, 153
wind 172–173, 206
  erosion 35, 40, 41, 46
  hurricanes 192–195
  speed 172
  tornadoes 196–199
  whirlwinds 200–201
windmills 173
winter 14, 15, 32, 98
Yangtze River, China 136
year 14

# Acknowledgements

Artwork supplied through the Art Agency by artists including Peter Bull and Myke Taylor. *Tyrannosaurus Rex* on p24 supplied by Jon Hughes and Russell Gooday.

Photo credits:
b = bottom, t = top, r = right, l = left, m = middle

Cover images:
Front: br Alexei Zaycev/iStock, bc Matthias Kulka/zefa/Corbis, cc Colin Keates/Getty Images, tc Gail Shumway/Getty Images, l Mario Cipollini/Getty Images.
Back: bc Daniel J. Cox/Getty Images, bl Frank Krahmer/Zefa/Corbis.
Spine: Digital Vision.

1 Digital Vision, 2–3 Dreamstime/Eugene Barzakovsky, 4–5 iStockphoto.com/Jan Will, 6tl Dreamstime.com/Boris Pamikov, 6ml Dreamstime.com/Dmytro Korolov, 6bl Dreamstime.com/Htuller, 6–7t Dreamstime.com/Yakobchuk, 6–7m Dreamstime.com/Wolfgang Amri, 6–7b iStockphoto.com/Andrew Martin, 7tl&bl Dreamstime.com/Gennadij Kurilin, 7tr Dreamstime.com/Stephen Mcsweeny, 7mr Dreamstime.com/Jose Fuente, 7br iStockphoto.com/Sergey Dubrovskiy, 8–9 Digital Vision, 10–11m NASA, 10 bl Dreamstime.com/Jinyoung Lee, 11tr Digital Vision, 11br iStockphoto.com/Soubrette, 12bl Dreamstime.com/Jeecis, 13tr Dreamstime.com/Ben Goode, 13br Dreamstime.com/Stephen Mcsweeny, 15tl Dreamstime.com/Jeanne Hatch, 15mr Corbis/Bernd Obermann, 15mlr Dreamstime.com/Geopappas, 15br Dreamstime.com/Koskins39, 16–17m Dreamstime.com/Sonya Etchison, 17b Dreamstime.com/Irochka, 18–19 NASA/JPL-Caltech, 19t Corbis/Bryan Allen, 19b Digital Vision, 20t Dreamstime.com/Ivan Cholakov, 20b iStockphoto.com/zbindere, 21b Dreamstime.com/Anthony Hall, 22 Dreamstime.com/Mark Bond, 23t Dreamstime.com/Ismael Montero, 23b Dreamstime.com/Kun Jiang, 25t Corbis/James L. Amos, 26 iStockphoto.com/Brett Hillyard, 27t Dreamstime.com/Joe Gough, 27b Dreamstime.com/Andrew Chambers, 29t Dreamstime.com/Musat Christian, 29b Dreamstime.com, 30t Dreamstime.com/Laurin Rinder, 30b Dreamstime.com/Nikhil Gangavane, 31t Dreamstime.com Dennis Sabo, 31b Dreamstime/Dennis Sabo, 32t Dreamstime.com/Maxfx, 32b Dreamstime.com/Roman Krochuk, 33t Dreamstime.com/Anthony Hathaway, 33b Dreamstime.com/Jan Martin Will, 34–35 Corbis/Herbert Spichtinger, 36t Dreamstime.com/Sebastian Kaulitzki, 36b Dreamstime.com, 37t Corbis/Ted Spiegel, 38t Dreamstime.com/Anatoly Tiplyashin, 38b Dreamstime.com/Charles Taylor, 39l Dreamstime.com/Peter Clark, 39r Dreamstime.com/Stephen Finn, 40t Dreamstime.com/David Lloyd, 40b Corbis/Robert Gill, 41t Dreamstime.com/Daniel Haller, 41b Dreamstime.com/Don Mace, 42t Dreamstime.com/David Lloyd, 42b iStockphoto.com/Carmen Martinez Banús, 43r Dreamstime.com/Rafael Laguillo, 43m Dreamstime.com/Andy Butler, 43m Dreamstime.com/Pavel Losevsky, 44t Dreamstime.com/Pancaketom, 44b Dreamstime.com/Jesse, 45t Dreamstime.com/Alexkalina, 45b Dreamstime.com/Aravindteki, 46 Dreamstime.com/Alena Yakusheva, 47t Dreamstime.com/Robert Cocquyt, 47m Dreamstime.com/Vlad Turchenko, 47b Dreamstime.com/David Watkins, 48l Dreamstime.com/Maxim Malevich, 48r Dreamstime.com/Kameel4u, 49t Dreamstime.com/Jerry Horn, 49b iStockphoto.com/Piotr Przeszlo, 50tl Corbis/Visuals Unlimited, 50tr Dreamstime.com/Andreasg, 50b Dreamstime.com/Kirill Bodrov, 51t Corbis/Bettmann, 51b Dreamstime.com/Oleg Fedorenko, 52l Corbis/Karen Michelmore, 52r Dreamstime.com/Ye Liew, 53t Dreamstime.com/Piotr Majka, 53m Corbis/Paul A. Souders, 53b Corbis/Jonathan Blair, 54t Dreamstime.com/Marat Hasanov, 55t Digital Vision, 55bl Dreamstime.com/Nicole Waring, 55bm Dreamstime.com/Evgeny Terentyev, 55br Dreamstime.com/Paul Butchard, 56l Dreamstime.com/Htuller, 57t Dreamstime.com/Alexandr Klochov, 57b iStockphoto.com/Donna Coleman, 58t Dreamstime.com/Pavel Gribkov, 58b Dreamstime.com/Phil Morley, 59t Dreamstime.com/Nikhil Gangavane, 59b Dreamstime.com/Alena Yakusheva, 60–61 Digital Vision, 62b Dreamstime.com/Sugarfree.sk, 63t Dreamstime.com/Marco Regalia, 63b Corbis/Michael S. Yamashita, 64b USGS/David Wieprecht, 65t Corbis/Jim Sugar, 65b USGS, 66–67 iStockphoto.com/Liz Leyden, 66t OAR/National Undersea Research Program (NURP), 66b Dreamstime.com/Simon Gurney, 67t Dreamstime.com/Keoni Dibelka, 68t USGS/Jim Nieland, 68b Corbis/Gary Braasch, 69t USGS/Lyn Topinka, 69b Dreamstime.com/Samuel Price, 70t Dreamstime.com/Victorpr, 70b Corbis/Sean Sexton, 71t Corbis/Les Stone/Sygma, 71b Corbis/Jacques Langevin/Sygma, 72t Corbis/Keren Su, 72b Dreamstime.com/Hugo Maes, 73t iStockphoto.com/Jeffrey Zavitski, 73b Dreamstime.com/Angela Cable, 74t Corbis/Roger Ressmeyer, 74b USGS/W. Chadwick, 75t Corbis/Les Stone/Sygma, 75b USGS/Gene Iwatsubo, 76 Dreamstime.com/Robert Paul Van Beets, 77t Corbis/Mark Downey/Lucid Images, 77b Corbis/TWPhoto, 78t NOAA/NGDC (National Geophysical Data Center), 78b Corbis/George Hall, 79t Corbis/Bernard Bisson/Sygma, 79b NGDC (National Geophysical Data Center), 80–81t Digital Vision, 80–81b iStockphoto.com/CK Lai, 81tr Corbis, 82t Corbis/Lisbon City Museum/Handout/Reuters, 82b USGS/Ralph O. Hotz, 83t Corbis/Peter Turnley, 83b Corbis/Warrick Page, 84t iStockphoto.com/James Benet, 84b Dreamstime.com/Adam Jastrzebowski, 85t Corbis/Reuters, 85b Dreamstime.com/Rafael Ramirez Lee, 86–87 iStockphoto.com/Vernon Wiley, 88t Corbis/Galen Rowell, 89b iStockphoto.com/Ogen Perry, 90 Dreamstime.com/Marc Johnson, 91t Dreamstime.com/Kevin Walsh, 91b iStockphoto.com/Warwick Lister-Kaye, 92–3 Dreamstime.com/Sascha Burkard, 93b Corbis/Skyscan, 94t Dreamstime.com/Jose Fuente, 94b Corbis/Robert Holmes, 95t iStockphoto.com/Robert Churchill, 95b Dreamstime.com/Jason Maeh, 96t Dreamstime.com/Alessandro Bolis, 96b Dreamstime.com/Andrew Millard, 97t Dreamstime.com/Robyn Mackenzie, 97b iStockphoto.com/Andrew Martin, 98t iStockphoto.com/Danny Warren, 99t iStockphoto.com/Marcella Francescangeli, 99b Dreamstime.com/Joeshmo, 100 Corbis/Steven Georges/Press-Telegram, 101tl Dreamstime.com/Mikel15, 101tr iStockphoto.com/Andreas Glossner, 101b iStockphoto.com/Nick Spannagel, 102t iStockphoto.com/Peter Archibald, 102b Dreamstime.com/Keith Young, 103t iStockphoto.com/Dmitry Pichugin, 103b Dreamstime.com/Jduggan, 104t iStockphoto.com/Ben Blankenburg, 104b Dreamstime.com/Stepanjezek, 105t Dreamstime.com/Mark Breck, 105b Corbis/Martin Harvey, 106–7 Dreamstime.com/Troy Farr, 106b Dreamstime.com/Joy Prescott, 107b Dreamstime.com/Reinhard Tiburzy, 108t Dreamstime.com/Spunky1234, 108b iStockphoto.com/Rey Rojo, 109t iStockphoto.com/Martin McCarthy, 109b iStockphoto.com/Bjorn Heller, 110t Dreamstime.com/Stephen Girimont, 110b Corbis/Arctic-Images, 111b Corbis/Johnathan Blair, 112–113 Digital Vision, 114t iStockphoto.com/Horst Puschmann, 115t iStockphoto.com/Roman Krochuk, 115b iStockphoto.com, 116–117 Dreamstime.com/Laurin Rinder, 116t Dreamstime.com/Laurie Weed, 117t Corbis/Ariel Skelley, 118t iStockphoto.com/Rob Jamieson, 119t iStockphoto.com/Milos Mokotar, 119b iStockphoto.com/Greg Brzezinski, 120t iStockphoto.com/Gregg Mack, 120b iStockphoto.com/Russell Gough, 121t Dreamstime.com/Ling Xia, 122l Jeff Schmaltz, MODIS Rapid Response Team, NASA/GSFC, 122b Wikipedia.org/Uryah, 123t iStockphoto.com, 123b Dreamstime.com/Jeffrey Banke, 124t Digital Vision, 124b USGS/National Center for EROS/NASA Landsat Project Science Office, 125t NASA, 125b Dreamstime.com/Gert Vrey, 126b iStockphoto.com,127t iStockphoto.com, 127b iStockphoto.com, 128t Corbis/Annie Griffiths Belt, 129t iStockphoto.com, 129b Corbis/Frank Lukasseck, 130t Dreamstime.com/Pierdelune, 130b Corbis/Ashley Cooper, 130–131m Dreamstime.com/Jhaviv, 131t Dreamstime.com/Aleksejs J., 131b Corbis/Pierre Vauthey, 132–133 Dreamstime.com/Vladimir Korostyshevskiy, 132m iStockphoto.com/Christopher Steer, 133t iStockphoto.com/Tom Grundy, 133m iStockphoto.com/Ian Scott, 134t iStockphoto.com/Edward Todd, 134b iStockphoto.com/Matthew Ragen, 135t iStockphoto.com/Alistair Scott, 135b Dreamstime.com/Olga Lyubkina, 136t Corbis/Hawes Alan/Sygma, 136b Corbis/Next Photo/Sygma, 137t iStockphoto.com/Geoffrey Hammond, 138–139 iStockphoto.com/James Steidl, 140t iStockphoto.com/Michael Braun, 141t iStockphoto.com/Natalia Diakov, 141b iStockphoto.com/Michael Steden, 142–143 Corbis/Rick Doyle, 143t Dreamstime.com/Jesse, 143m Dreamstime.com/Elisalocci, 144l iStockphoto.com, 144b iStockphoto.com/Michelle Reaves, 145t Dreamstime.com/Carolyne Pheora, 146t Edward Simkins, 146–147 iStockphoto.com/Rey Rojo, 147t Dreamstime.com/Nico Smit, 148t NASA, 148b iStockphoto.com/Vera Bogaerts, 149t Dreamstime.com/Wolfgang Amri, 149b iStockphoto.com/Trina Denner, 150l iStockphoto.com/Tammy Peluso, 151tr iStockphoto.com/Adrian Baddeley, 151m Dreamstime.com/Andrea Leone, 151b Dreamstime.com/Ian Scott, 152b Corbis/Douglas P. Wiilson/Frank Lane Picture Agency, 153t Corbis/Bob Gomel, 154m iStockphoto.com/Chris Zwaenepoel, 155t Dreamstime.com/Kiminnb, 156t Corbis/Ralph White, 156b OAR/National Undersea Research Program (NURP)/Woods Hole Oceanographic Inst., 157b Corbis/Ralph White, 158t Dreamstime.com/Pete Favelle, 158b Corbis/Tim Davis, 159b Corbis/Bettmann, 160t iStockphoto.com/Luis Pedrosa, 160b Corbis/Michael Freeman, 161t iStockphoto.com/Patricia Hofmeester, 161b Digital Vision, 162t Corbis/Bettmann, 162b iStockphoto.com/Kenneth C. Zirkel, 163t Corbis/Stephen Frink, 163b Dreamstime.com/Tatiana Edrenkina, 164–165 iStockphoto.com/Hans F. Meier, 166t Digital Vision, 167t Corbis/Nawang Sherpa/Bogati/ZUMA, 167b Dreamstime.com/Elena Elisseeva, 168t Dreamstime.com/Robyn Mackenzie, 168–169b Dreamstime.com/Eugene Barzakovsky, 169t iStockphoto.com/Barry Crossley, 169b iStockphoto.com, 170tl Dreamstime.com/Elena Schweite, 170tr Dreamstime.com/Aleksandr Ugorenkov, 170b Dreamstime.com/Millan, 171t Dreamstime.com/Paula Stephens, 171b Dreamstime.com/Boris Pamikov, 172t Dreamstime.com/Johann Helgason, 172b Dreamstime.com/Danijel Micka, 173l Dreamstime.com/Kurt, 173r Dreamstime.com/Dageldog, 174–175 Dreamstime.com/John Wollwerth, 174m Dreamstime.com/Kmitu, 175t iStockphoto.com, 175b iStockphoto.com/David Cannings-Bushell, 176–177t Dreamstime.com/Oleksandr Staroseltsev, 176b Dreamstime.com/Demydenko Myhailo, 177t Dreamstime.com/Yakobchuk, 177b Dreamstime.com/Jorge Salcedo, 178b Dreamstime.com/Douglas Hall, 179tr Dreamstime.com/Jörg Jahn, 179b Dreamstime.com/Dmytro Korolov, 180t Dreamstime.com/Viktor Ostashevskyy, 180b Dreamstime.com/Carolyne Pehora, 181t Dreamstime.com/Kjuby, 181b iStockphoto.com/Daniel Stein, 182l Dreamstime.com/Paul Moore, 182–183 Dreamstime.com/Roger Degen, 183t Dreamstime.com/Don Mace, 183m Corbis/Howard Burditt/Reuters, 184–185 Dreamstime.com/Vova Pomortzeff, 185t Dreamstime.com/Dmytro Korolov, 185b Corbis/Philippe Lissac/Godong, 186–187 iStockphoto.com/Sergey Dubrovskiy, 186b Corbis/Nik Wheeler, 187t Corbis/Wolfgang Kaehler, 187b iStockphoto.com/David P. Lewis, 188tl Dreamstime.com/Armin Rose, 188b Dreamstime.com/Millan, 189t iStockphoto.com/Lisa F. Young, 189b Dreamstime.com/Miflippo, 190–191 Corbis/Carson Ganci/Design Pics, 192b Jacques Descloitres, MODIS Rapid Response Team, NASA/GSFC, 193t Corbis/Daniel Aguilar/Reuters, 193b Melissa Ann Janssen/FEMA, 194t Marvin Nauman/FEMA, 194b Jocelyn Augustino/FEMA, 195t Bob McMillan/FEMA, 195b Mark Wolfe/FEMA, 196–197 Corbis/Eric Nguyen, 197t Mark Wolfe/FEMA, 198b John Plisich/ FEMA, 199t Andrea Booher/FEMA, 199b Corbis/Jim Reed, 200–201 iStockphoto.com/Christopher Walker, 200t iStockphoto.com/Vladimir Kondrachov, 201tl Dreamstime.com/Erik Lam, 201tr iStockphoto.com/Alexei Zaycev, 201b Dreamstime.com/Nadeem Khawer/epa, 202b iStockphoto.com/Mark Rose, 202–203 Digital Vision, 203b National Park Service, 204t Dreamstime.com/Alexander Zhiltsov, 204b iStockphoto.com/Michael Madsen, 205t Dreamstime.com/Lars Lentz, 205b Corbis/Reuters, 206t Corbis/Reuters, 207t Corbis, 207b Crystal Payton/FEMA, 208t Dreamstime.com/Gennadij Kurilin, 208–209 Dreamstime.com/Kathy Wynn, 209t Dreamstime.com/Anna Chelnokova, 209b Dreamstime.com/Georgy Pchemyan, 210t iStockphoto.com/Silvia Jansen, 210b iStockphoto.com/Rick Hinson, 211m Corbis/Jim Reed, 212b Digital Vision, 213t Dreamstime.com/Bertrandb, 213b iStockphoto.com/Jan Will, 214t Dreamstime.com/Kanu Suguro, 214b iStockphoto.com/Ana Abejon, 215l Dreamstime.com/Showface, 215r Dreamstime.com/Lukasz Fus.